VOL. 132

COUNTRY ROCK

ISBN 978-1-4234-9812-4

Visit Hal Leonard Online at
www.halleonard.com

GUITAR NOTATION LEGEND

THE MUSICAL STAFF shows pitches and rhythms and is divided by bar lines into measures. Pitches are named after the first seven letters of the alphabet.

TABLATURE graphically represents the guitar fingerboard. Each horizontal line represents a string, and each number represents a fret.

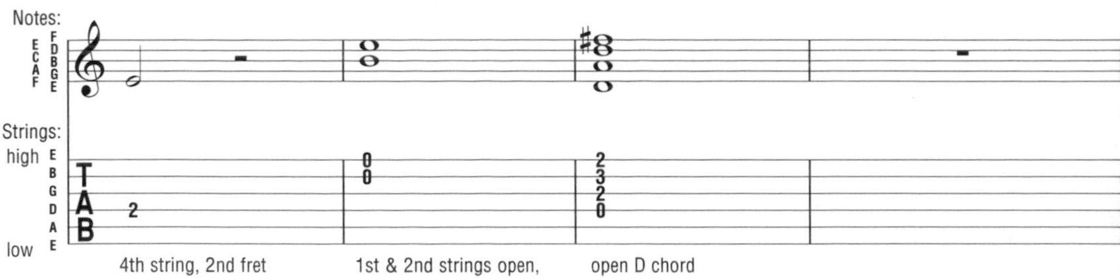

HALF-STEP BEND: Strike the note and bend up 1/2 step.

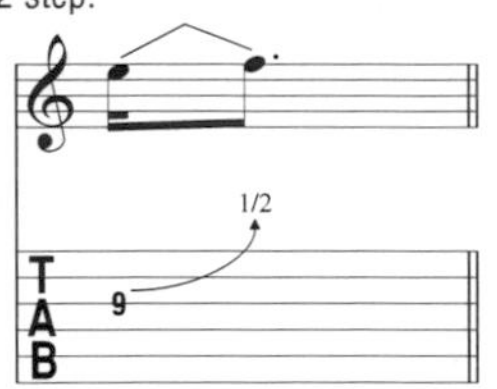

WHOLE-STEP BEND: Strike the note and bend up one step.

GRACE NOTE BEND: Strike the note and immediately bend up as indicated.

SLIGHT (MICROTONE) BEND: Strike the note and bend up 1/4 step.

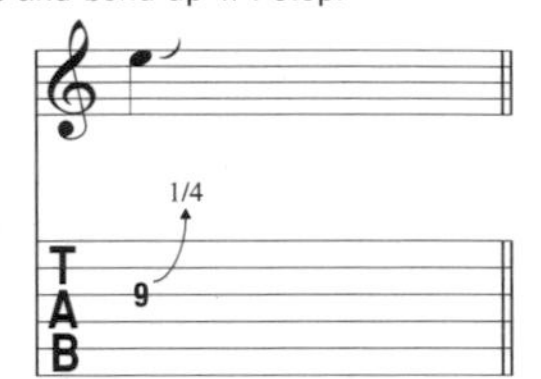

BEND AND RELEASE: Strike the note and bend up as indicated, then release back to the original note. Only the first note is struck.

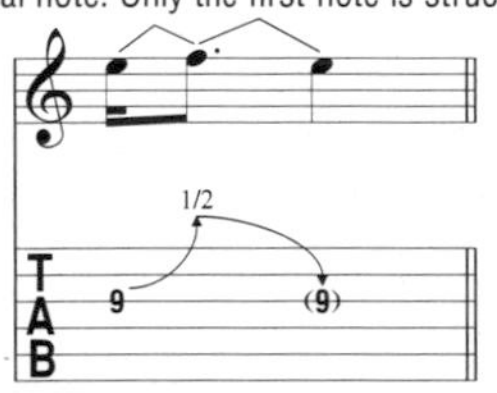

PRE-BEND: Bend the note as indicated, then strike it.

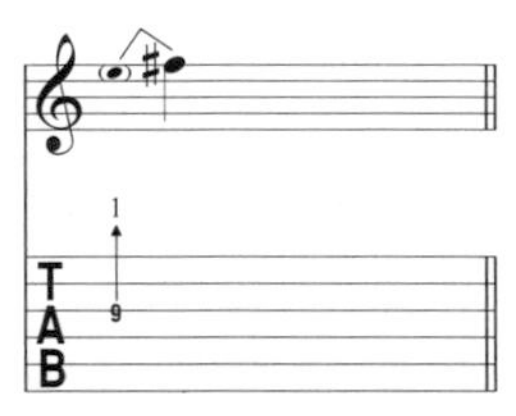

VIBRATO: The string is vibrated by rapidly bending and releasing the note with the fretting hand.

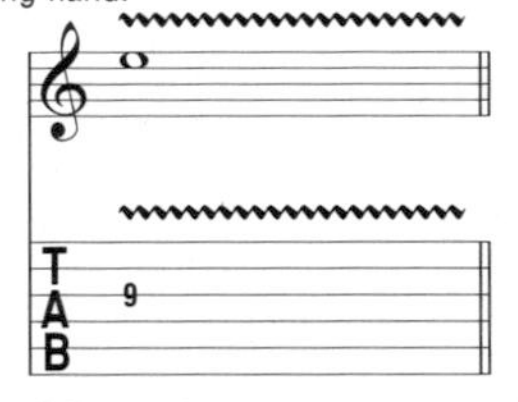

PALM MUTING: The note is partially muted by the pick hand lightly touching the string(s) just before the bridge.

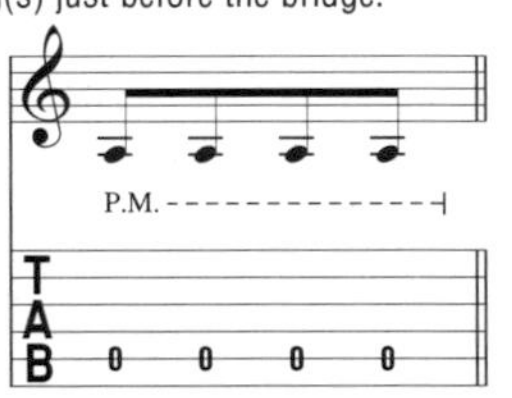

HAMMER-ON: Strike the first (lower) note with one finger, then sound the higher note (on the same string) with another finger by fretting it without picking.

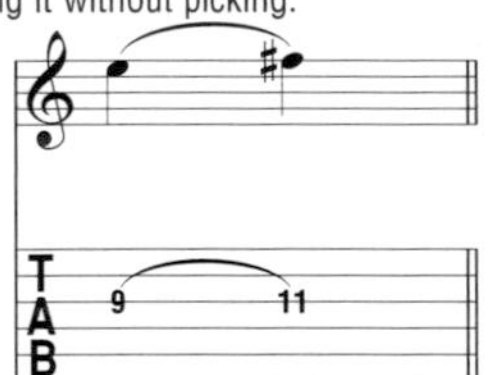

PULL-OFF: Place both fingers on the notes to be sounded. Strike the first note and without picking, pull the finger off to sound the second (lower) note.

LEGATO SLIDE: Strike the first note and then slide the same fret-hand finger up or down to the second note. The second note is not struck.

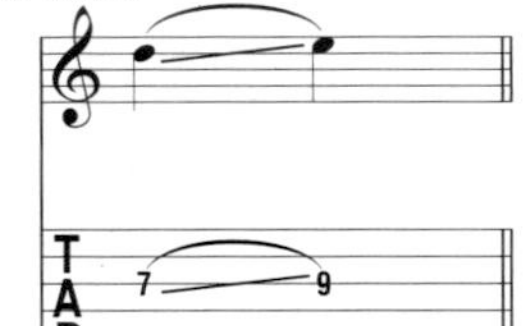

SHIFT SLIDE: Same as legato slide, except the second note is struck.

TRILL: Very rapidly alternate between the notes indicated by continuously hammering on and pulling off.

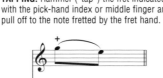

TAPPING: Hammer ("tap") the fret indicated with the pick-hand index or middle finger and pull off to the note fretted by the fret hand.

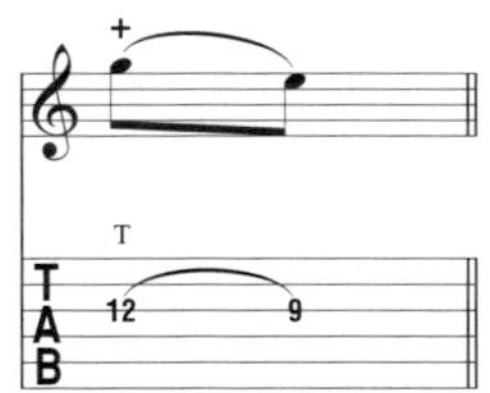

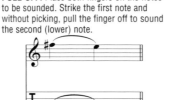

NATURAL HARMONIC: Strike the note while the fret-hand lightly touches the string directly over the fret indicated.

PINCH HARMONIC: The note is fretted normally and a harmonic is produced by addi the edge of the thumb or the tip of the index finger of the pick hand to the normal pick atta

TREMOLO PICKING: The note is picked as rapidly and continuously as possible.

VIBRATO BAR DIVE AND RETURN: The pitch of the note or chord is dropped a specified number of steps (in rhythm), then returned to the original pitch.

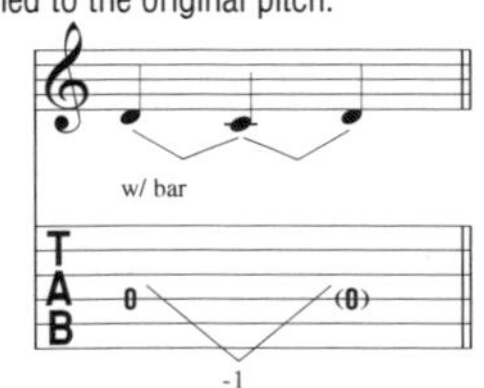

VIBRATO BAR SCOOP: Depress the bar just before striking the note, then quickly release the bar.

VIBRATO BAR DIP: Strike the note and then immediately drop a specified number of steps, then release back to the original pitch

Additional Musical Definitions

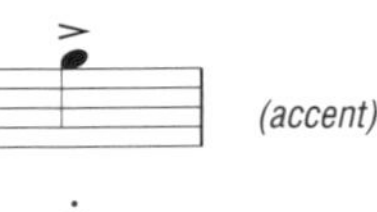

(accent) • Accentuate note (play it louder).

(staccato) • Play the note short.

D.S. al Coda • Go back to the sign (𝄋), then play until the measure marked "***To Coda***," then skip to the section labelled "**Coda**."

D.C. al Fine • Go back to the beginning of the song and play until the measure marked "***Fine***" (end).

Fill • Label used to identify a brief melodic figure which is to be inserted into the arrangement.

N.C. • Harmony is implied.

• Repeat measures between signs.

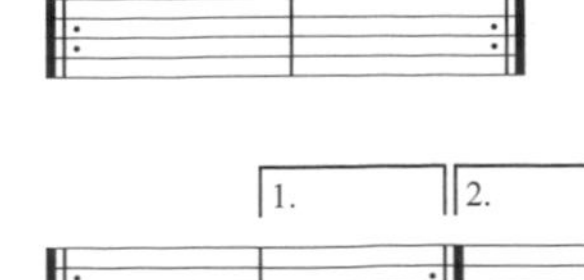

• When a repeated section has different endings, play the first ending only the first time and the second ending only the second time.

CONTENTS

Drivin' My Life Away

Words and Music by Eddie Rabbit, Even Stevens and David Malloy

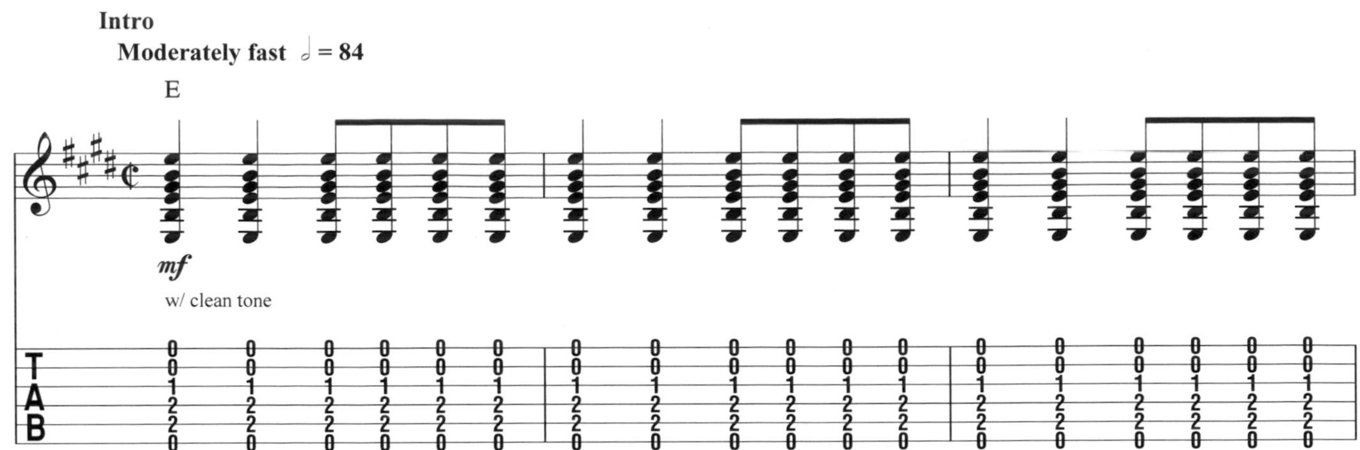
Intro
Moderately fast 𝅗𝅥 = 84
E
mf
w/ clean tone
T
A
B

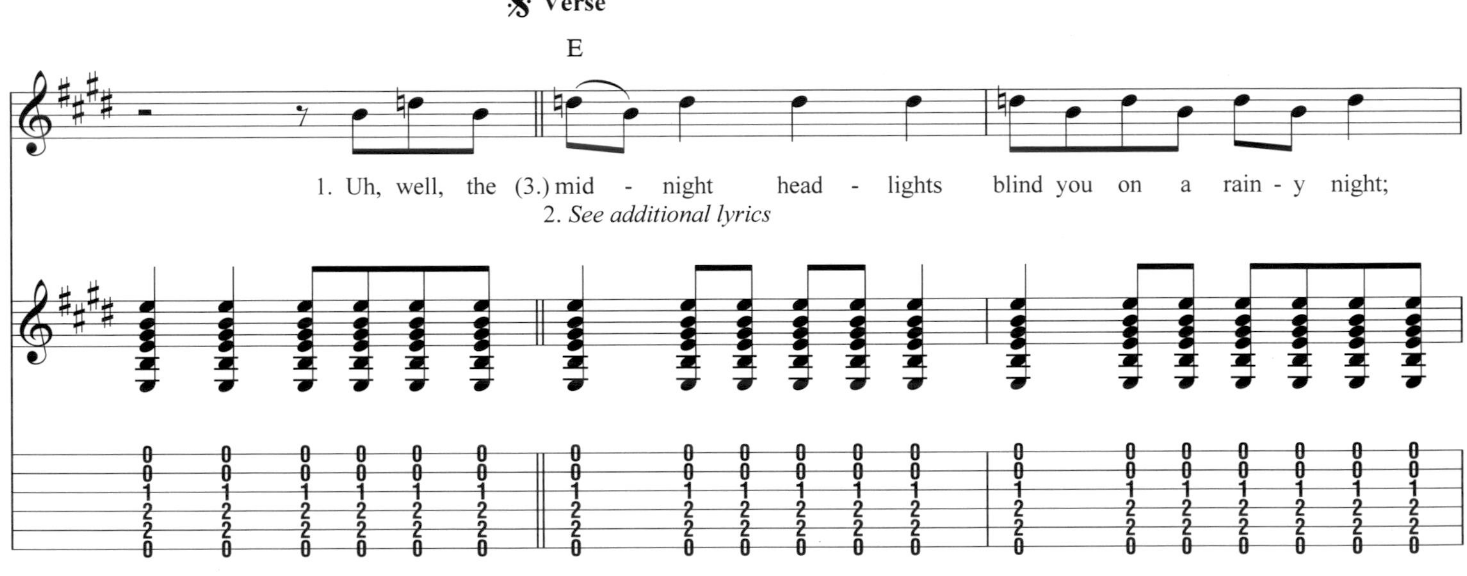
𝄋 Verse
E
1. Uh, well, the (3.) mid - night head - lights blind you on a rain - y night;
2. See additional lyrics

A
steep grade up a - head, slow me down, mak - in' no time,

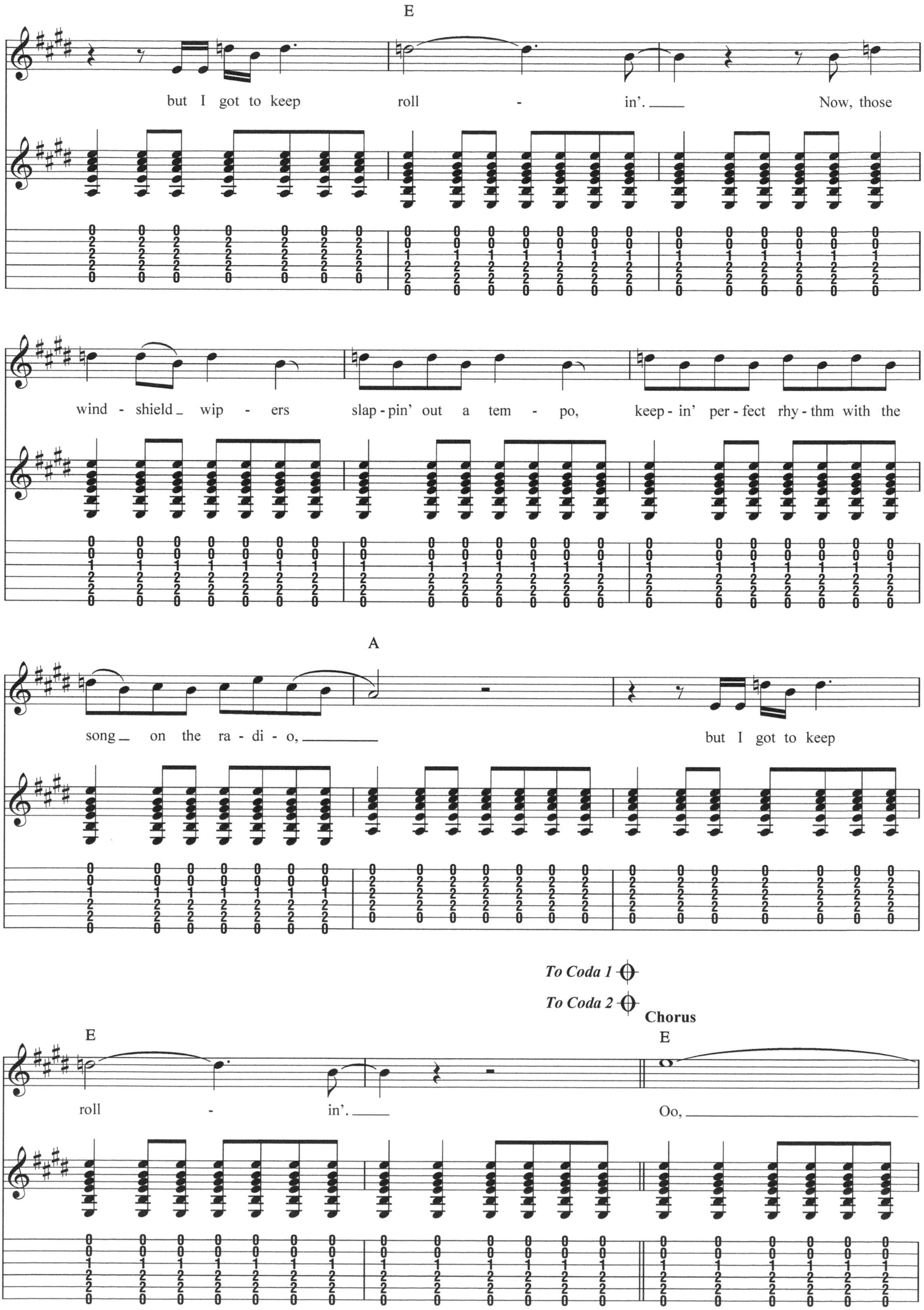

E

but I got to keep roll - in'. Now, those

wind - shield wip - ers slap - pin' out a tem - po, keep - in' per - fect rhy - thm with the

A

song on the ra - di - o, but I got to keep

To Coda 1 𝄌

To Coda 2 𝄌

Chorus

E E

roll - in'. Oo,

D

I'm driv - in' my life a - way, look - in' for a

A E

bet - ter way for me.

w/ slight dist.

P.M.

Oo, I'm driv - in' my

P.M.

1/2

D A

life a - way, look - in' for a sun - ny day.

Interlude

C♯m B A

G E

D.S. al Coda 1

2. Well, the

let ring

let ring

Coda 1

Chorus

E D

Oo, I'm driv - in' my life a - way,

w/ dist.

A E

look - in' for a bet - ter way for me.

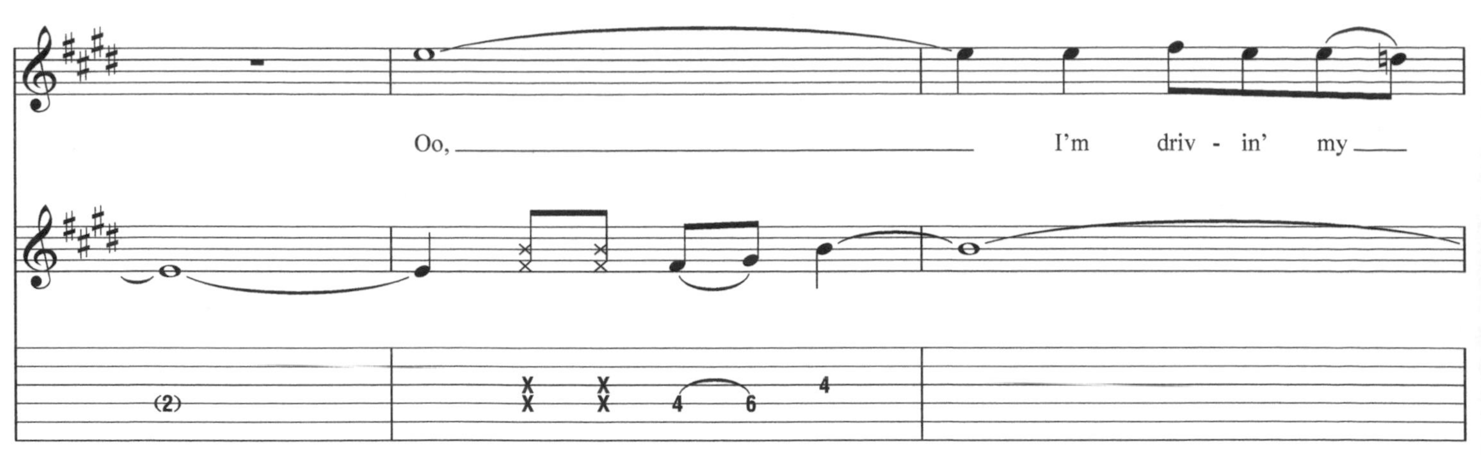

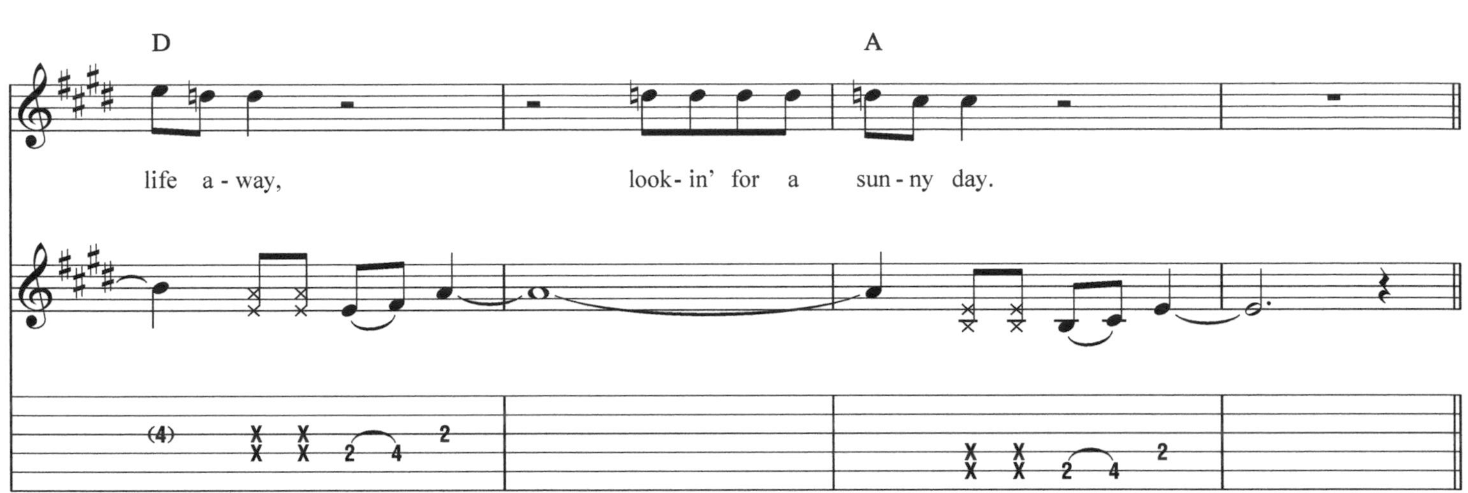

Interlude

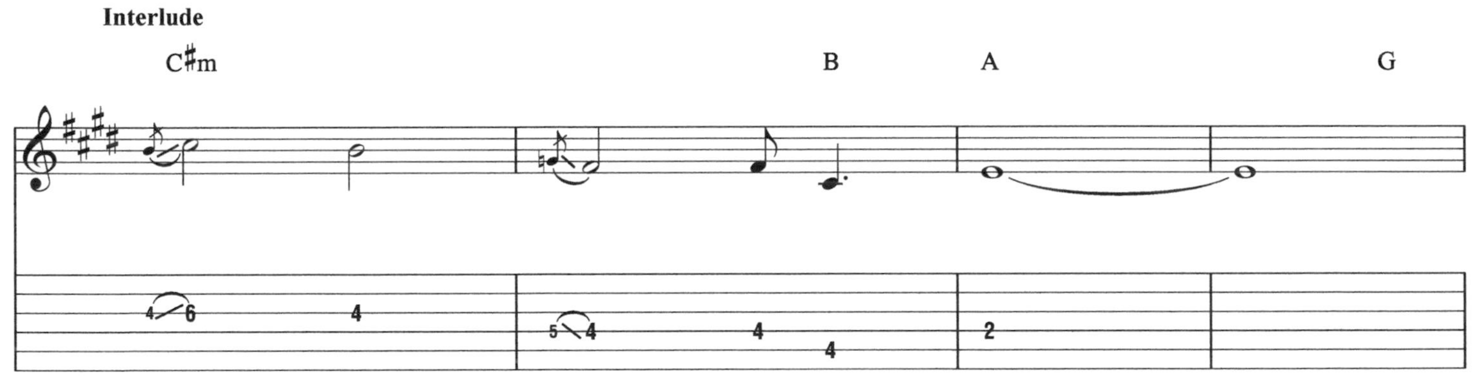

D.S. al Coda 2

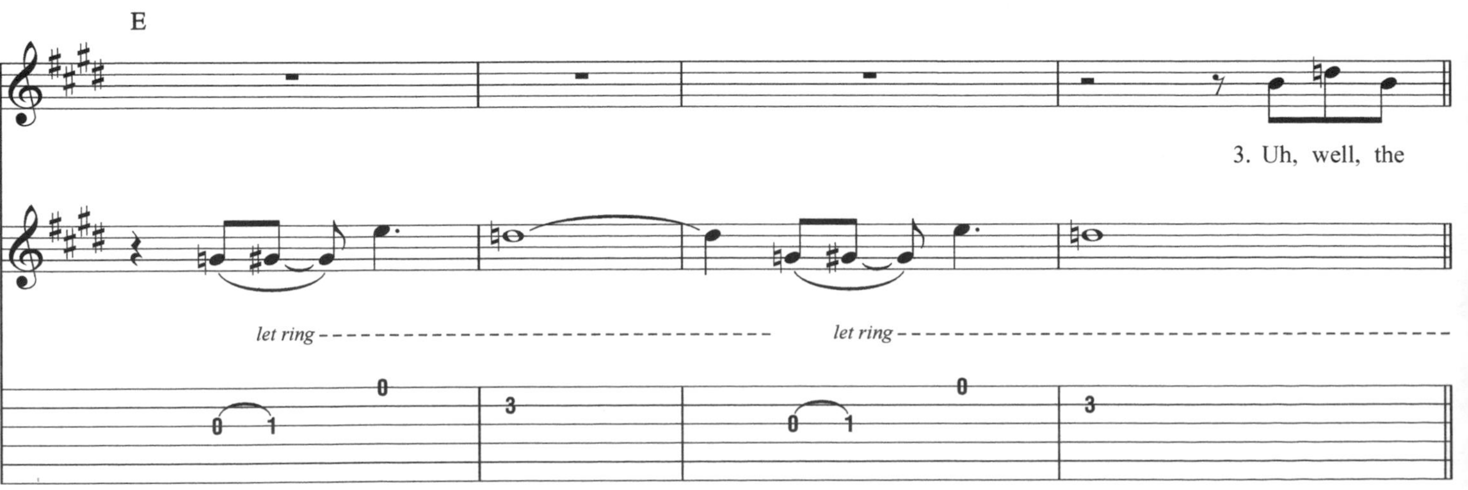

Coda 2
Chorus
E
D
Oo, I'm driv - in' my life a - way,
w/ dist.
A
E
look - in' for a bet - ter way for me.
D
Oo, I'm driv - in' my life a - way,
A
look - in' for a sun - ny day.

E
Oo,
D
A
I'm driv-in' my life a-way, look-in' for a bet-ter way
E
for me.
Oo,
D
I'm driv-in' my life a-way, look-in' for a

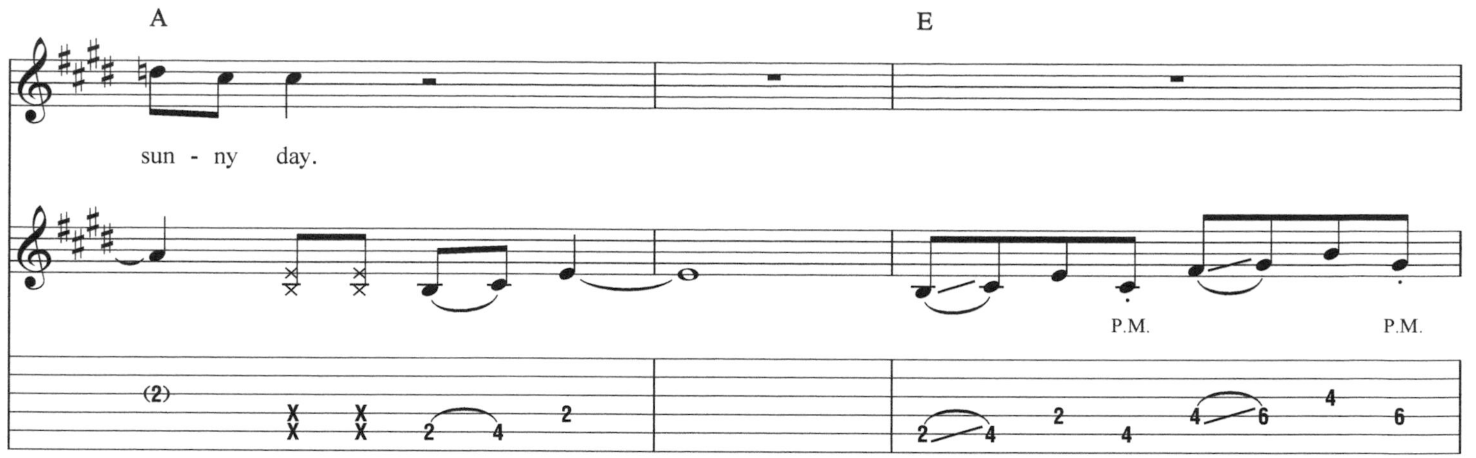

Additional Lyrics

2. Well, the truck stop cutie comin' on to me,
Try'n' to talk me into a ride, said I wouldn't be sorry.
But she was just a baby.
Hey waitress, pour me another cup of coffee.
Pop it down, jack me up, shoot me out, flyin' down the highway.
Lookin' for the mornin'.

East Bound and Down

from the Universal Film SMOKEY AND THE BANDIT

Words and Music by Jerry Reed and Dick Feller

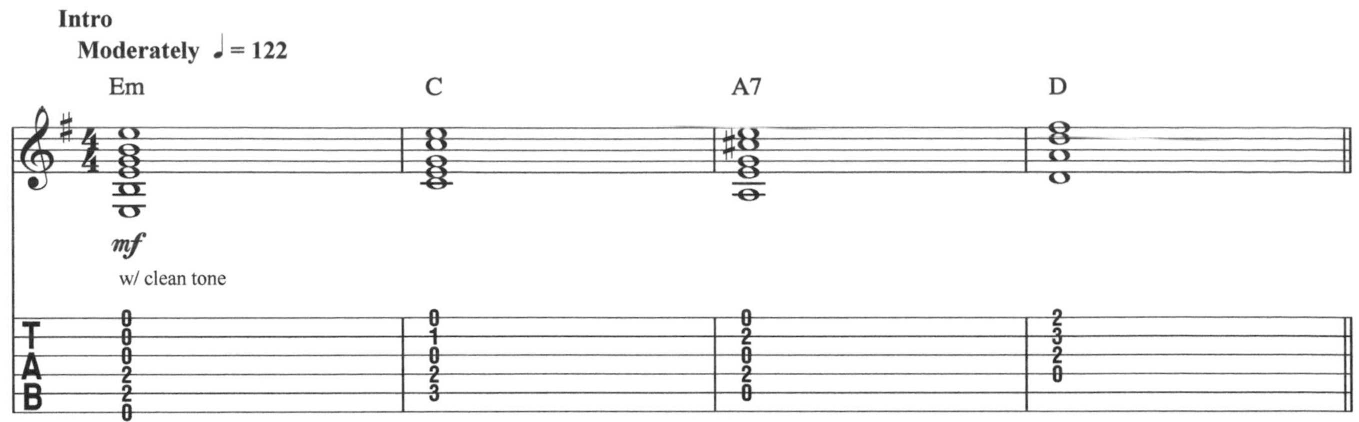

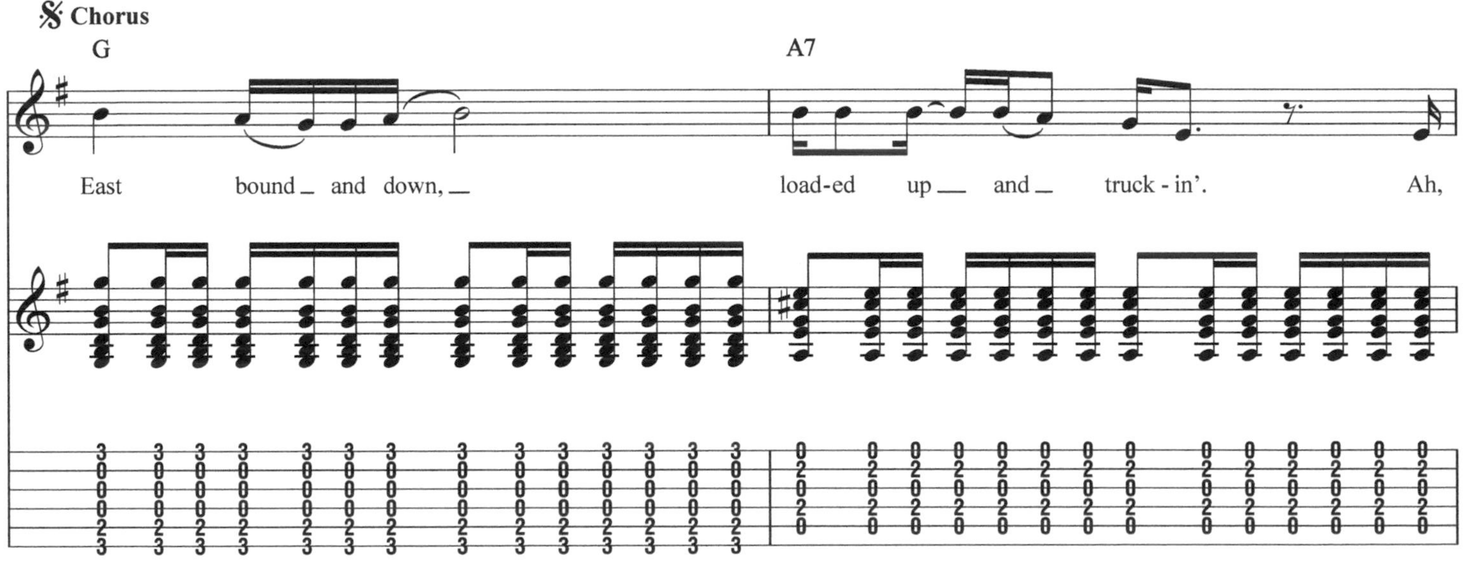

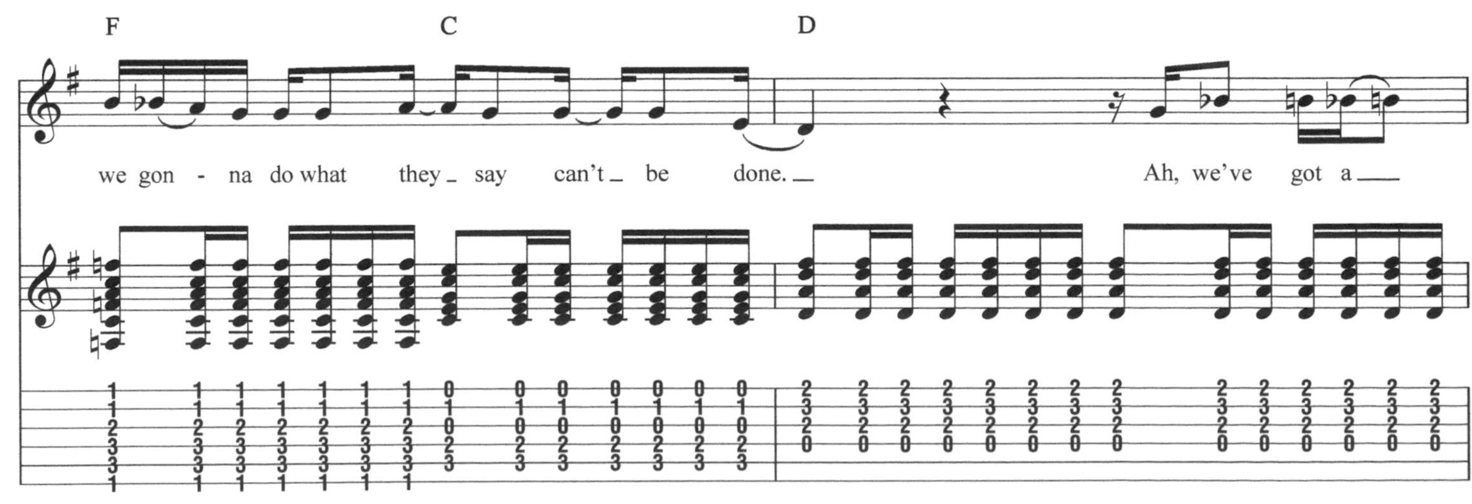

G
A7
long way to go and a short time to get there. I'm
To Coda 1
F
D
G
east bound, just watch ol' Ban - dit run.
1. Keep your
2. See additional lyrics
Verse
Em
C
foot hard on the ped - al. Son, nev - er mind them brakes. Let it
A7
B7
Em
B7
all hang out 'cause we got a run to make. The boys are

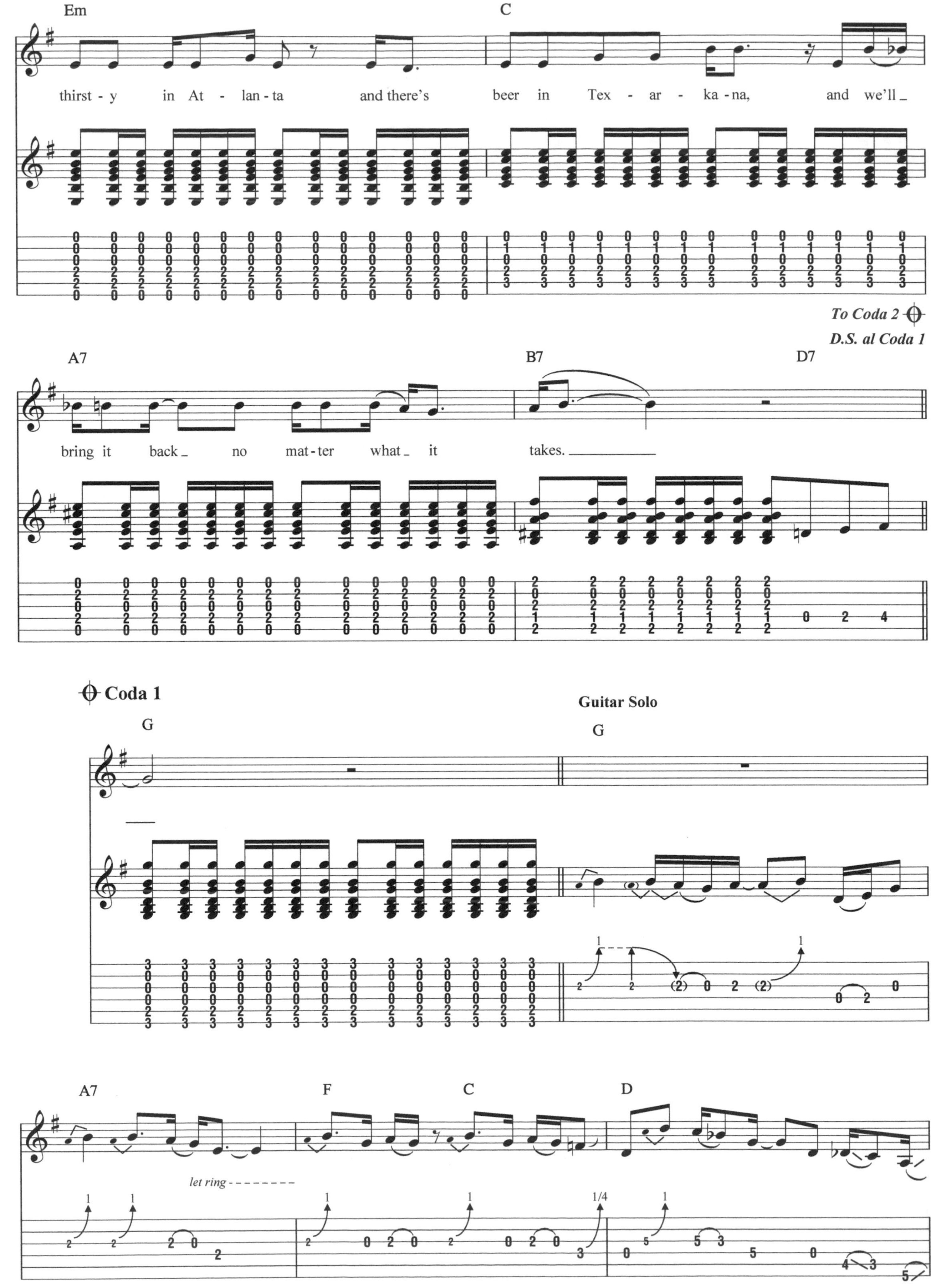

Em
C
thirst - y in At - lan - ta and there's beer in Tex - ar - ka - na, and we'll
To Coda 2
D.S. al Coda 1
A7
B7
D7
bring it back no mat - ter what it takes.
Coda 1
Guitar Solo
G
G
A7
F
C
D
let ring

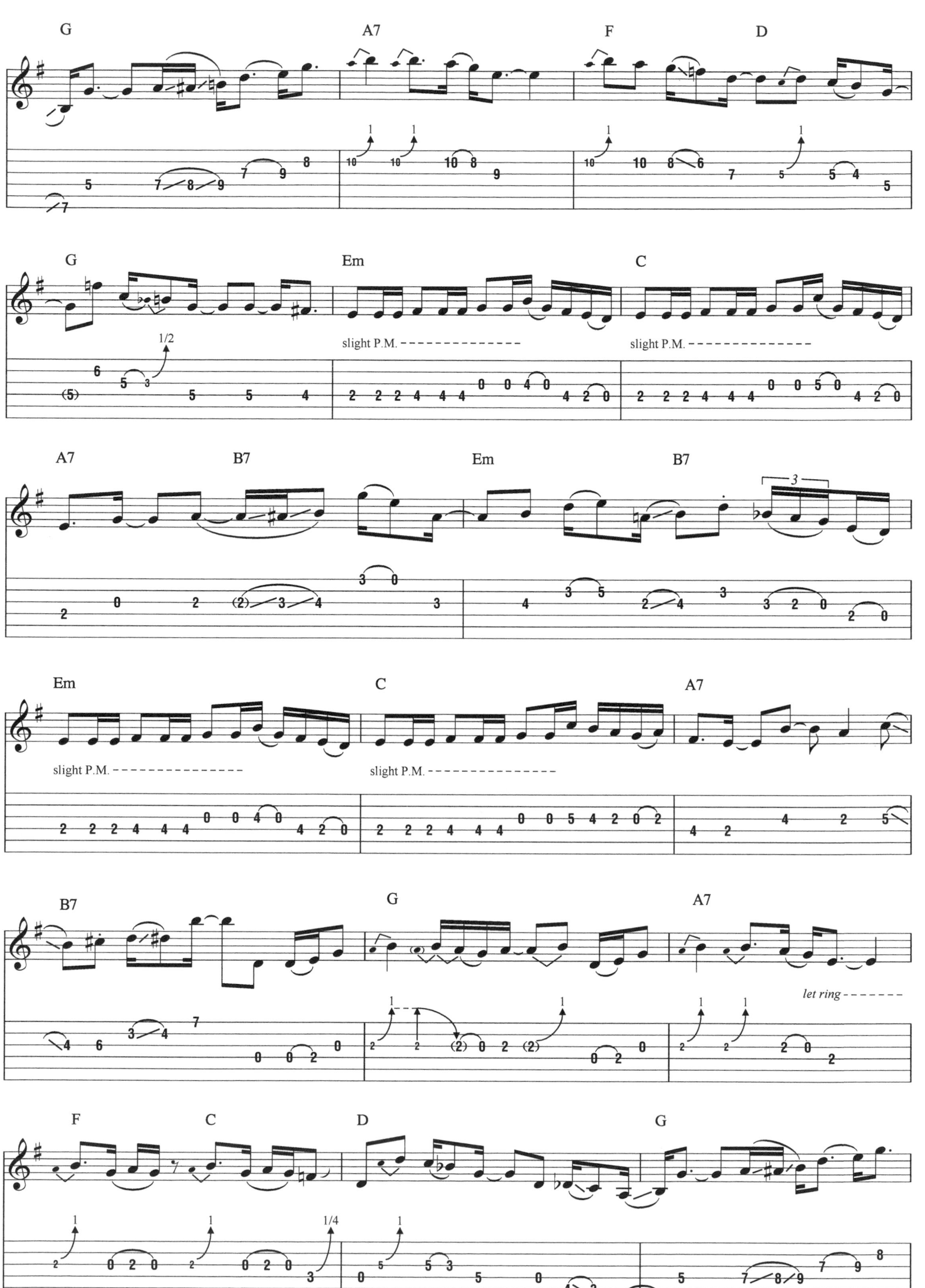
G
A7
F
D
G
Em
C
slight P.M.
slight P.M.
A7
B7
Em
B7
Em
C
A7
slight P.M.
slight P.M.
B7
G
A7
let ring
F
C
D
G

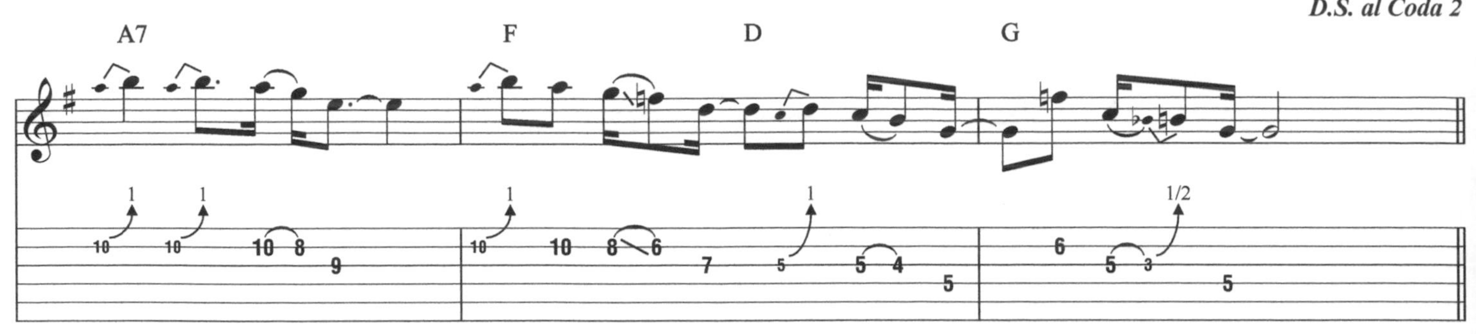
D.S. al Coda 2
A7
F
D
G

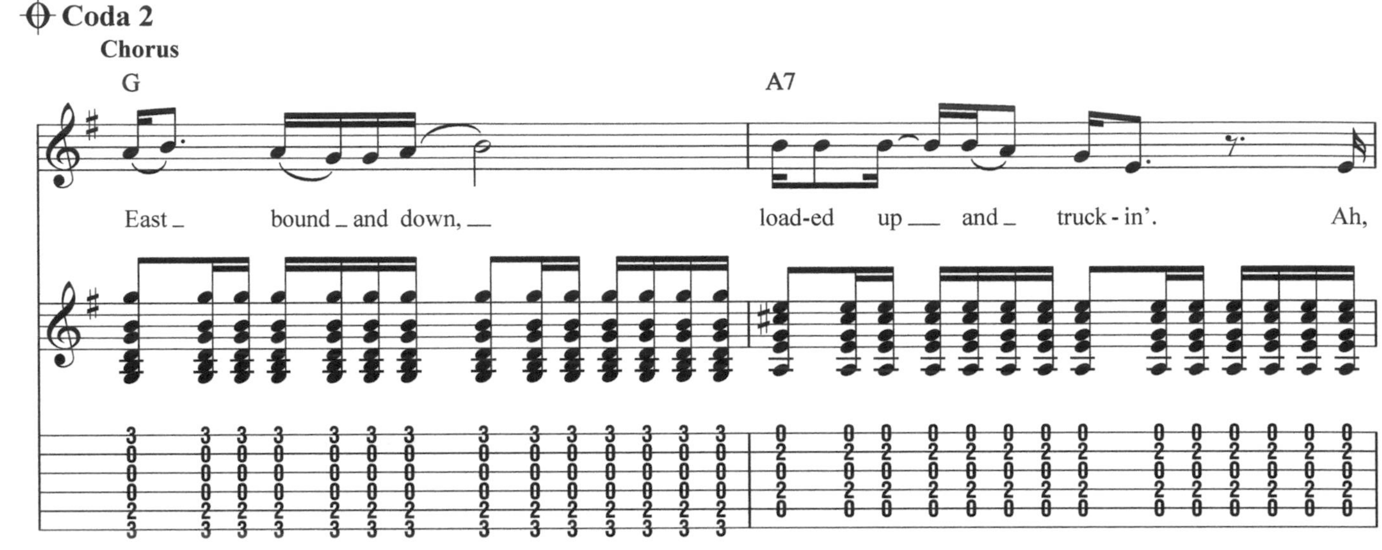
Coda 2
Chorus
G
A7
East _ bound _ and down, _
load-ed up _ and _ truck - in'.
Ah,

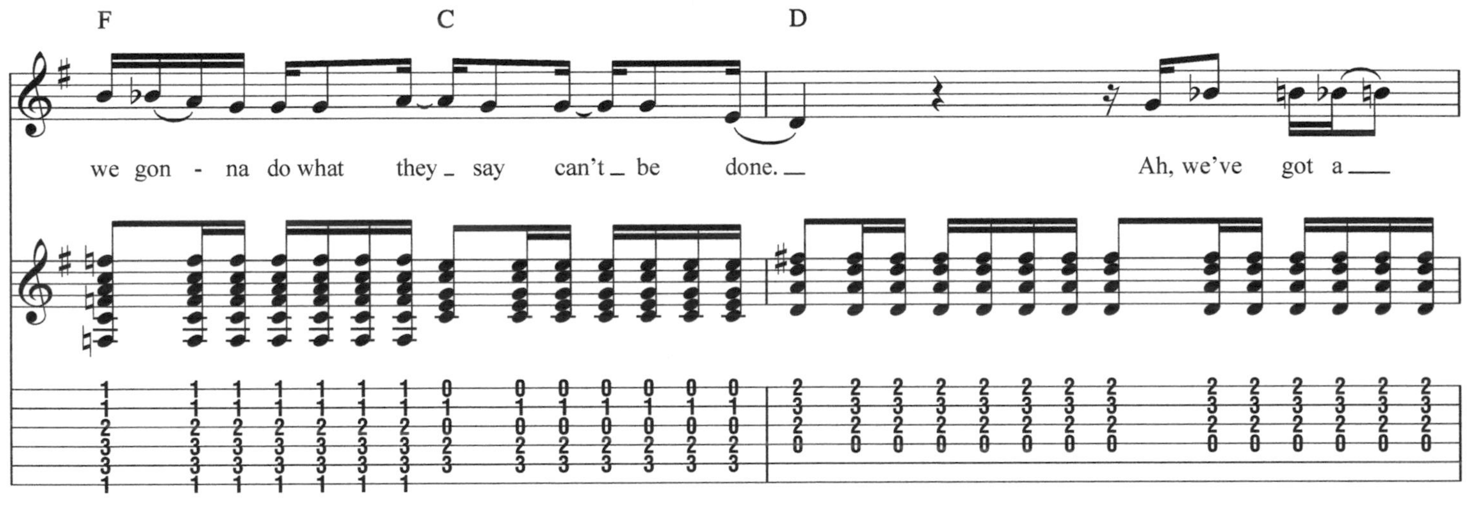
F
C
D
we gon - na do what they _ say can't _ be done. _
Ah, we've got a ___

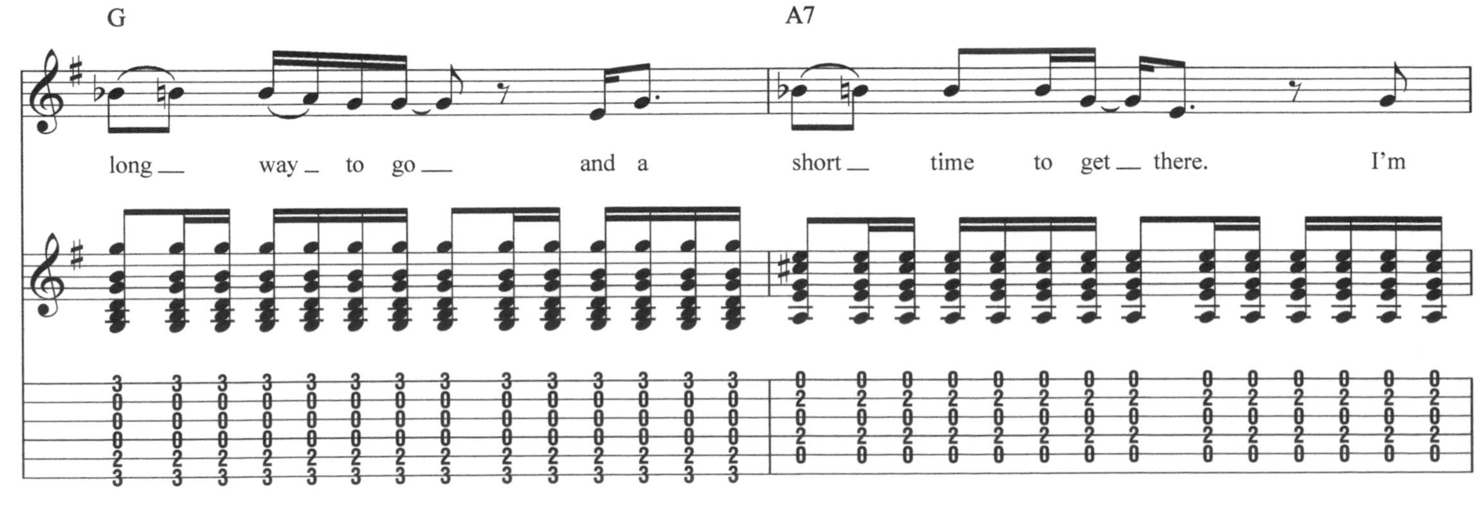
G
A7
long _ way _ to go _ and a
short _ time to get _ there.
I'm

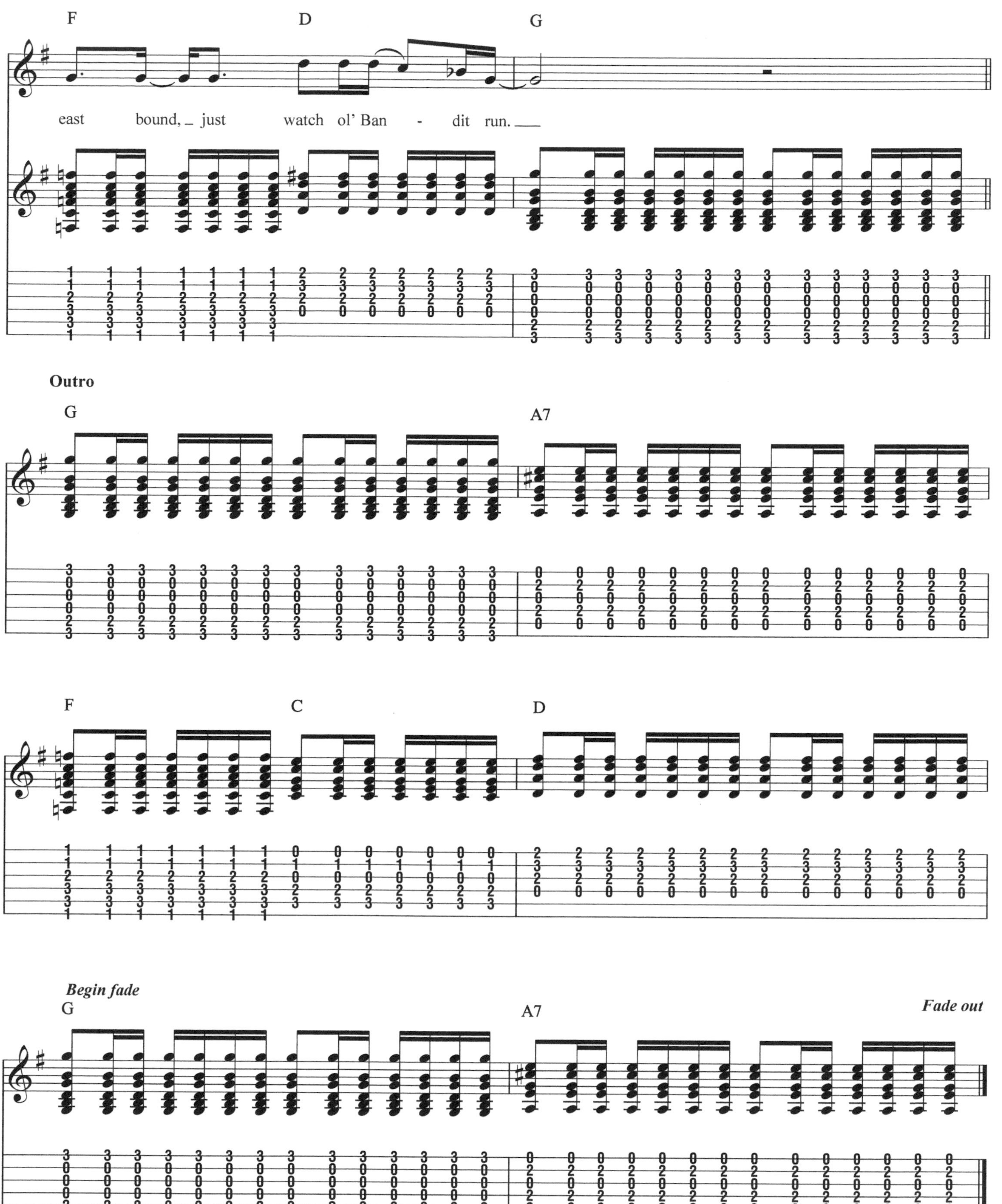

Additional Lyrics

2. Old Smokey's got them ears on, he's hot on your trail.
And he ain't gonna rest till you're in jail.
So, you've got to dodge him, you've got to duck him.
You got to keep that diesel truckin'.
Just put the hammer down and give it hell.

Guitars, Cadillacs

Words and Music by Dwight Yoakam

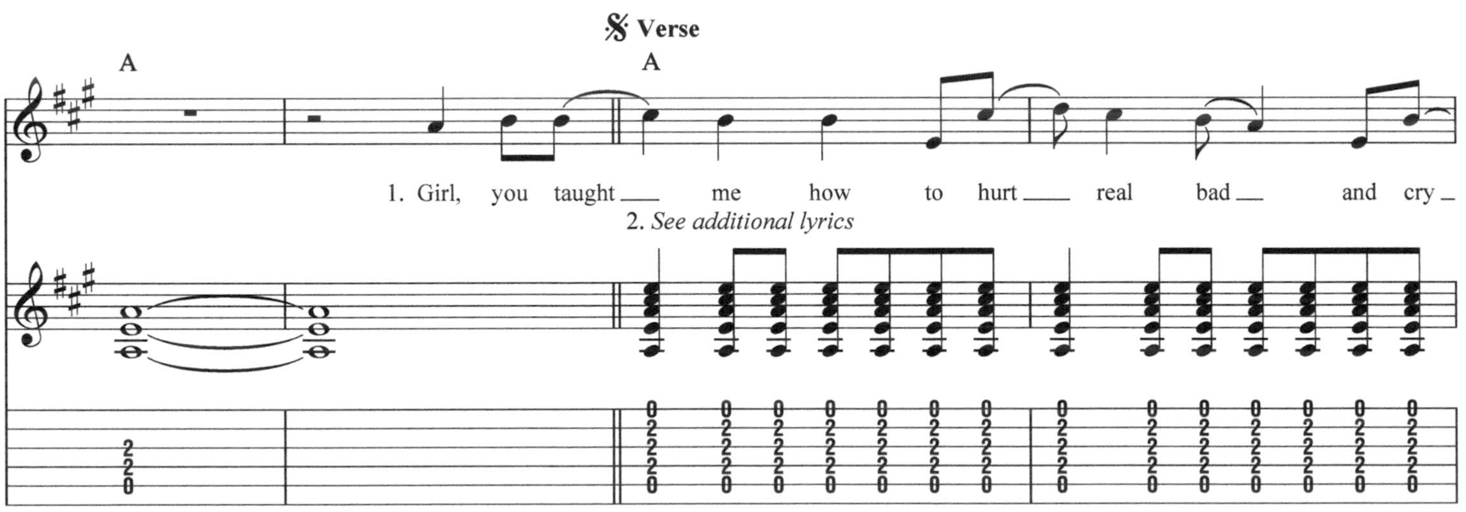

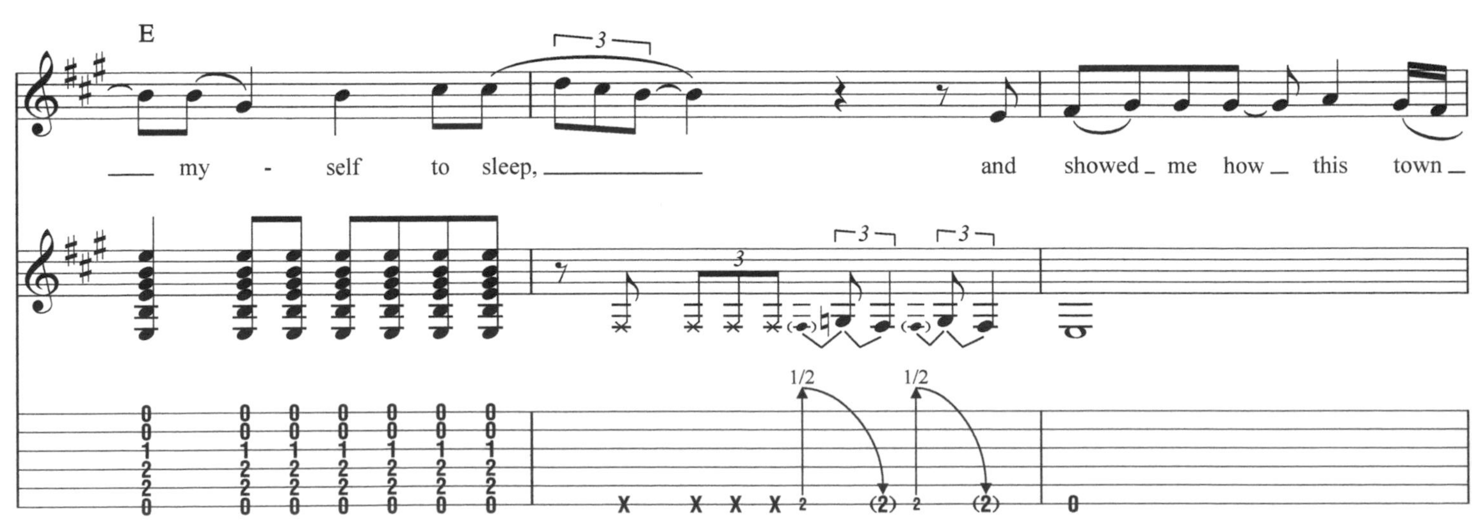

A
can shat - ter dreams.
An - oth - er les -
1/2
1/2
E
- son 'bout a na - ive fool who came to Bab - y - lon and
1/2
1/2
A
found out that the pie don't taste so sweet.
Now it's
1/2
1/2
Chorus
A
E
gui - tars, Ca - dil - lacs, hill - bil - ly mu - sic, lone -

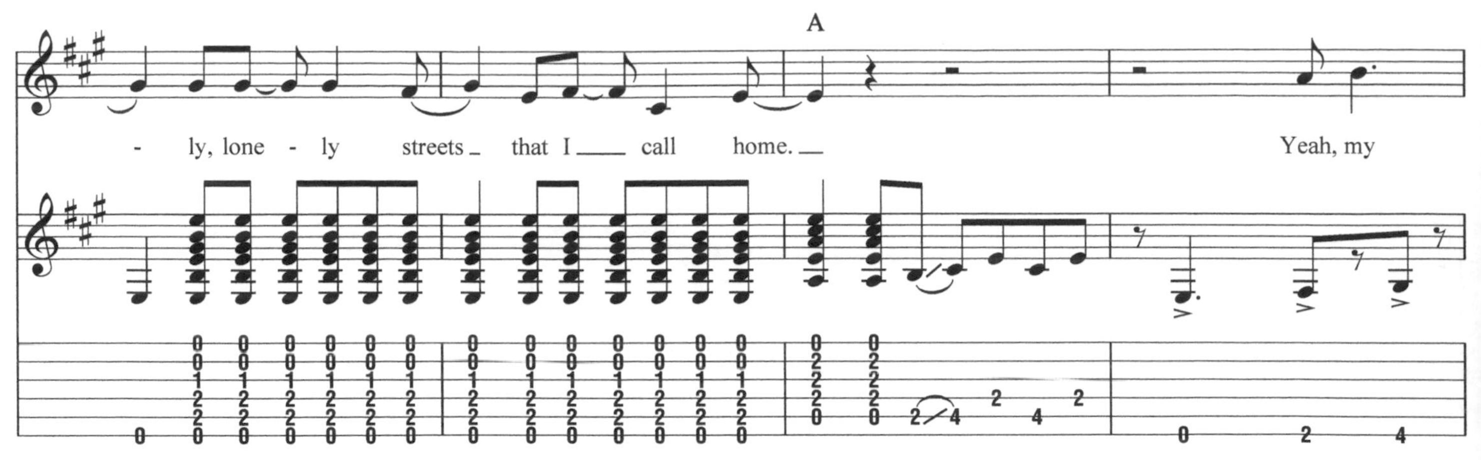
A
- ly, lone - ly streets that I call home.
Yeah, my

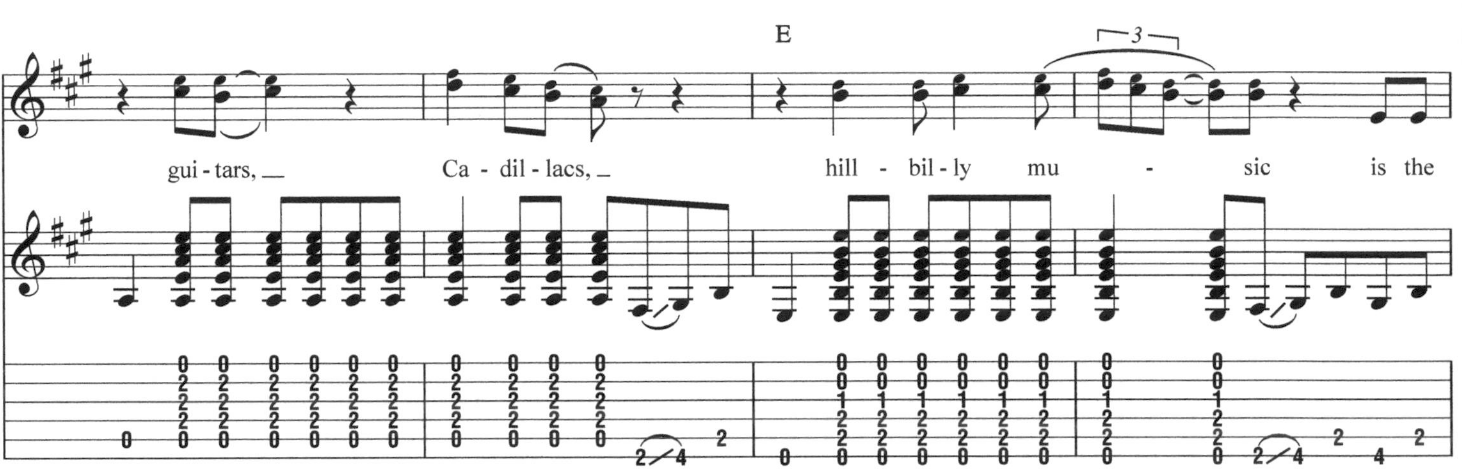
E
gui - tars,
Ca - dil - lacs,
hill - bil - ly mu - sic is the

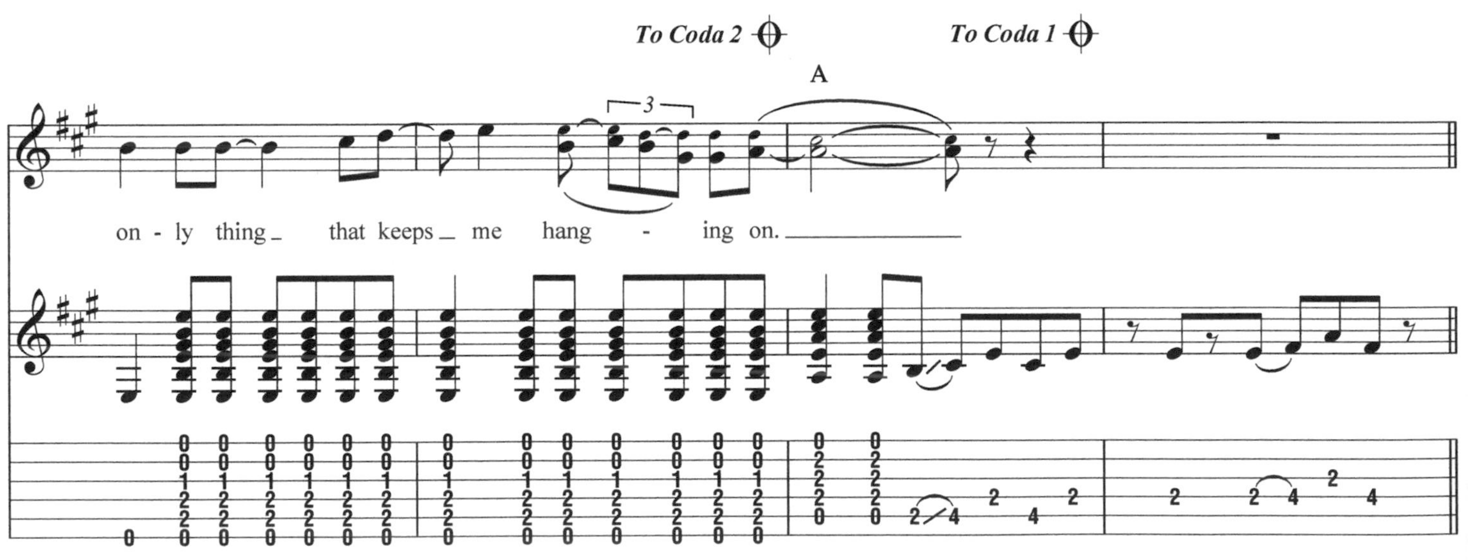
To Coda 2
To Coda 1
A
on - ly thing that keeps me hang - ing on.

Guitar Solo

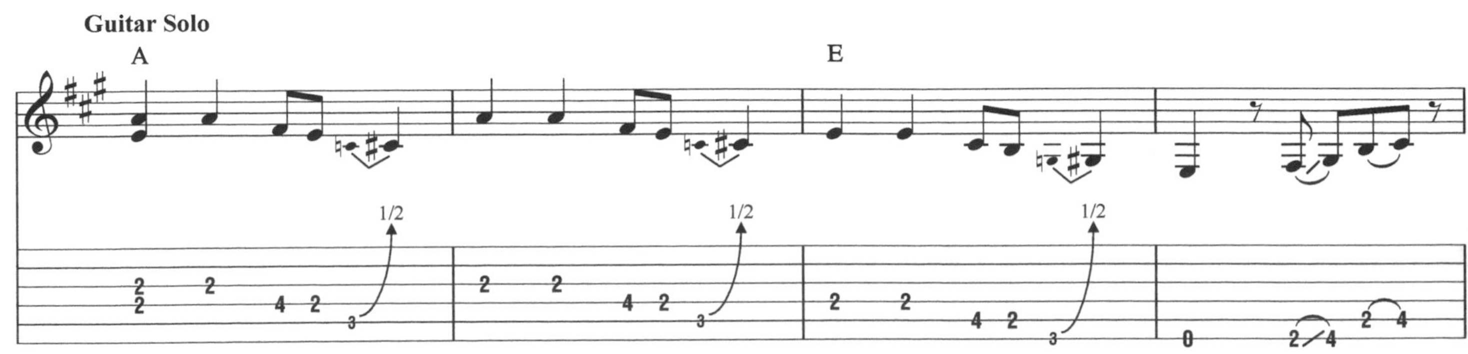
A
E
1/2
1/2
1/2

A
1/2
1/2

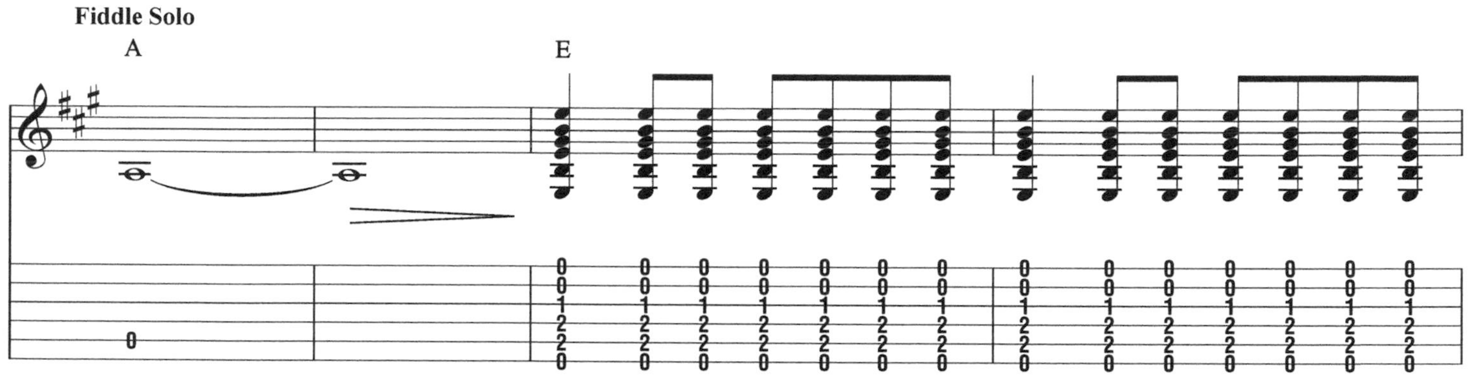
Fiddle Solo
A
E

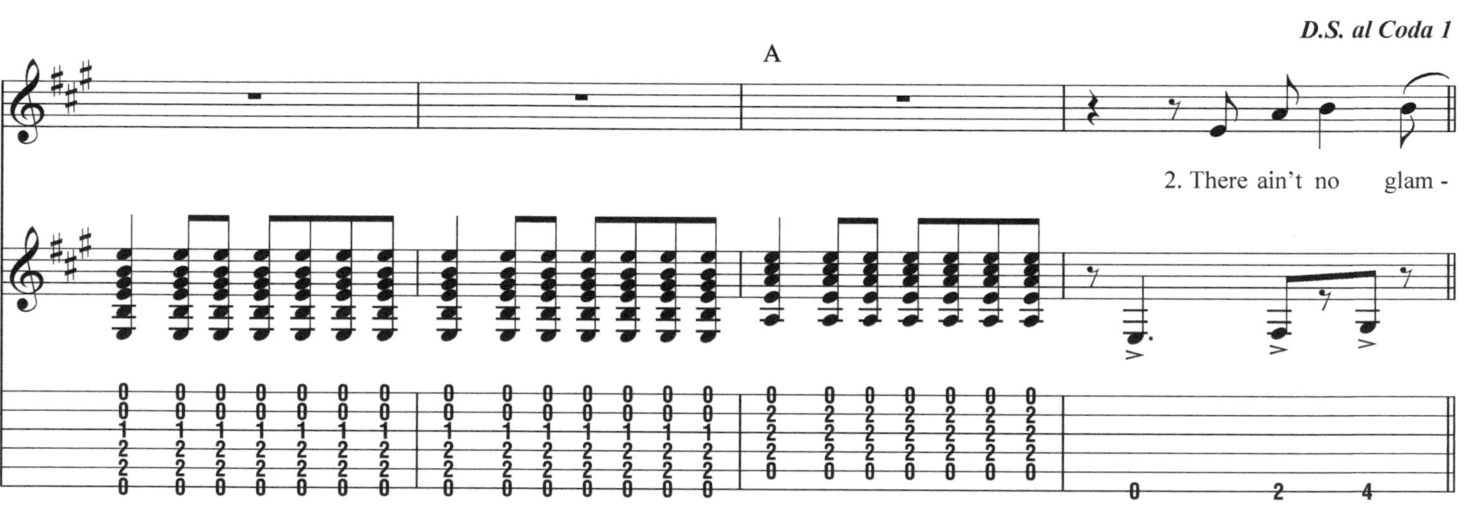
D.S. al Coda 1
A
2. There ain't no glam -

Coda 1
Guitar Solo
A
w/ pick & fingers
let ring
let ring
let ring
let ring
1

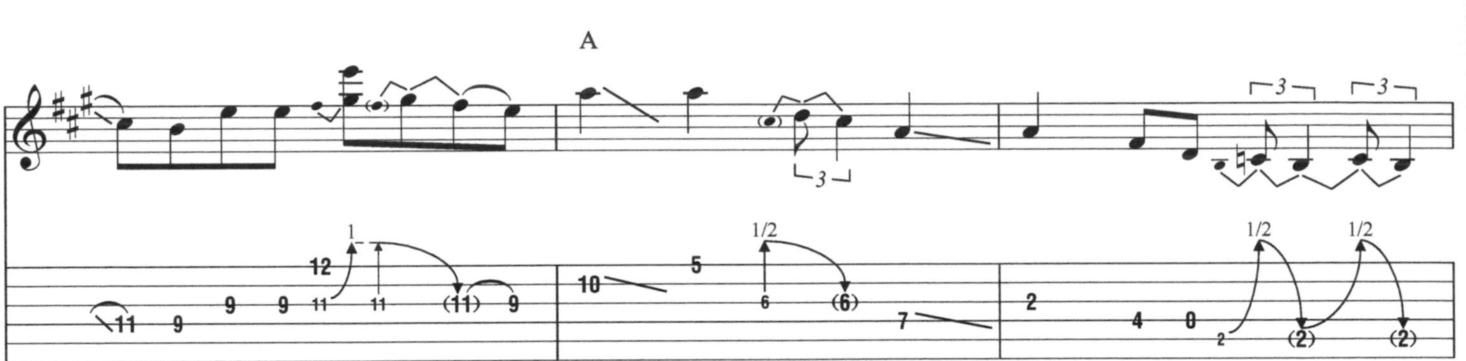

Fiddle Solo

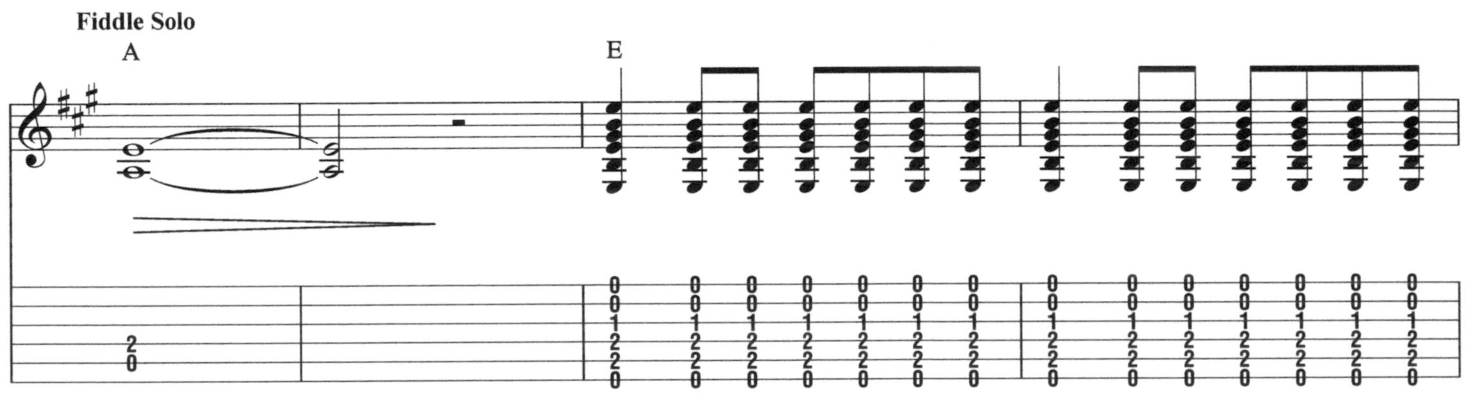

D.S.S. al Coda 2

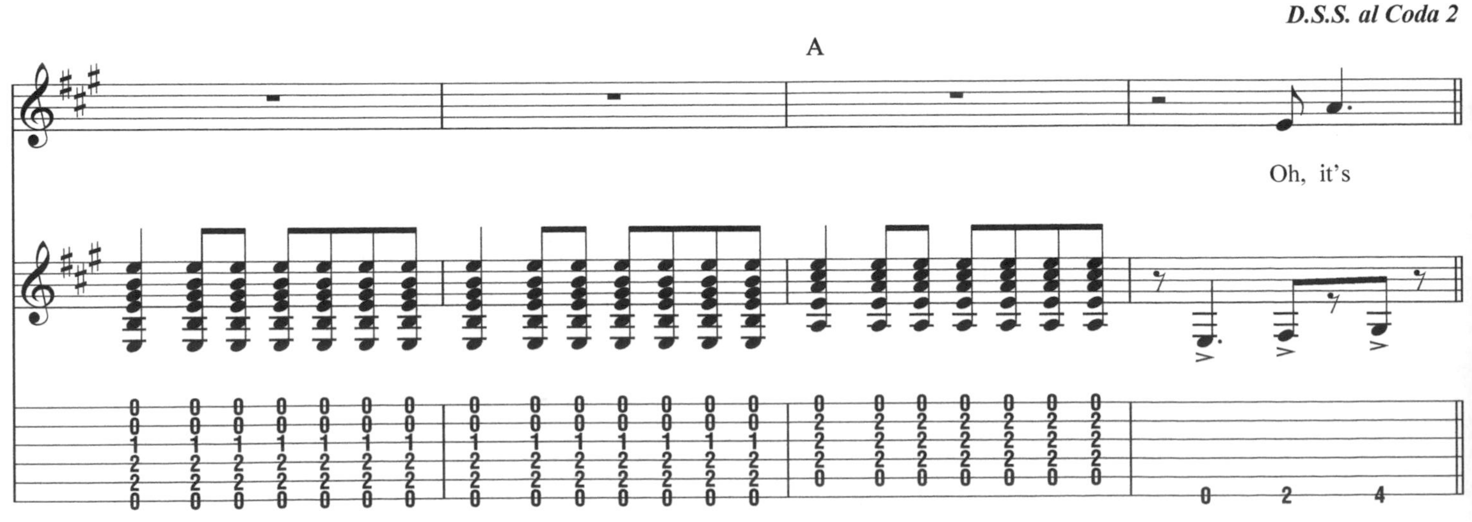

Coda 2

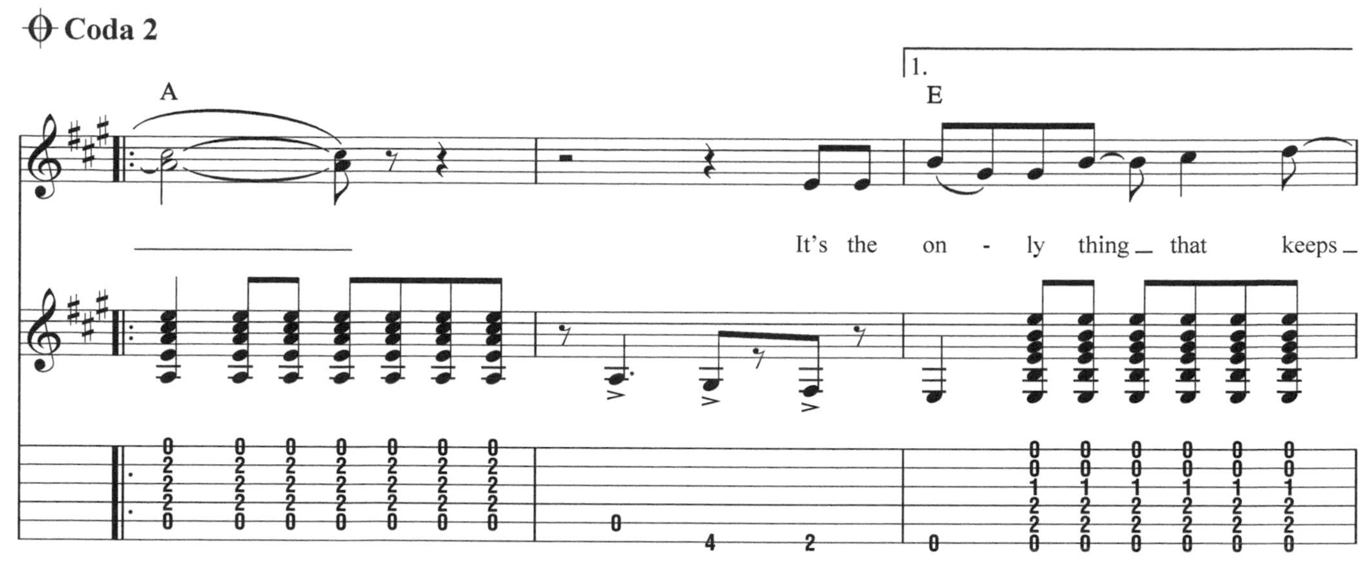

A
1.
E
It's the on - ly thing that keeps

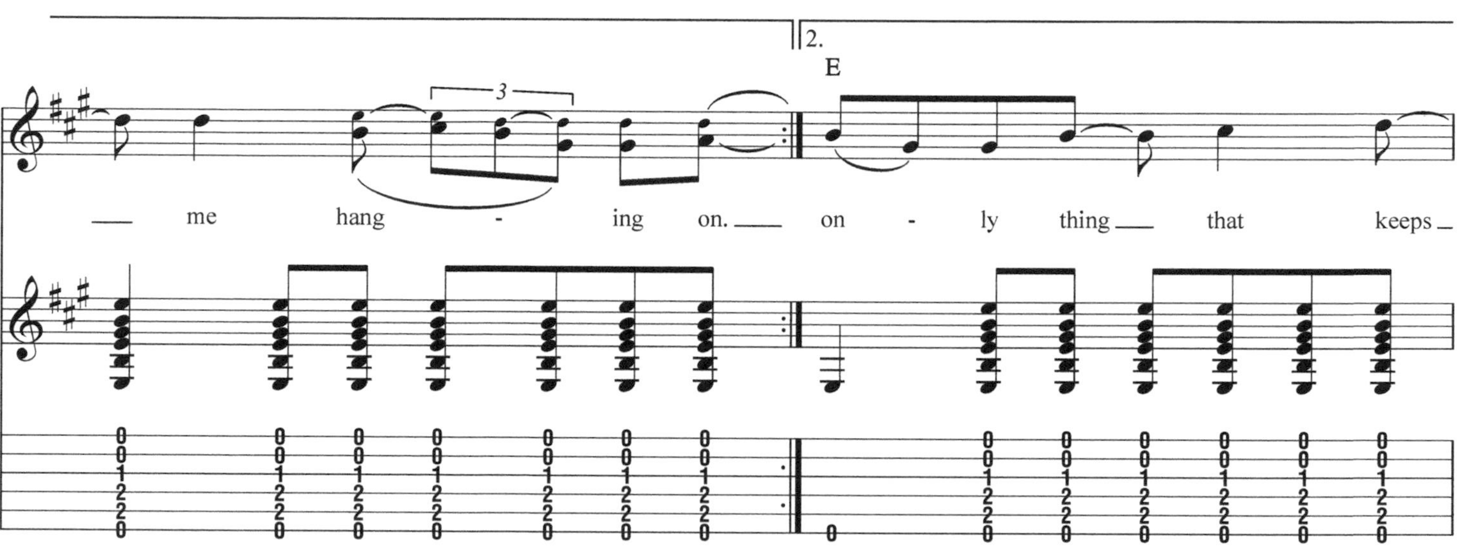

2.
E
me hang - ing on. on - ly thing that keeps

A
me hang - ing on.
1/2
1/2
1/2

Additional Lyrics

2. There ain't no glamour in this tinsel land of lost and wasted lives.
Painful scars are all that's left of me.
Oh, but thank you, girl, for teaching me brand new ways to be cruel.
If I can find my mind now, I guess I'll just leave. And it's...

Here's a Quarter
(Call Someone Who Cares)
Words and Music by Travis Tritt

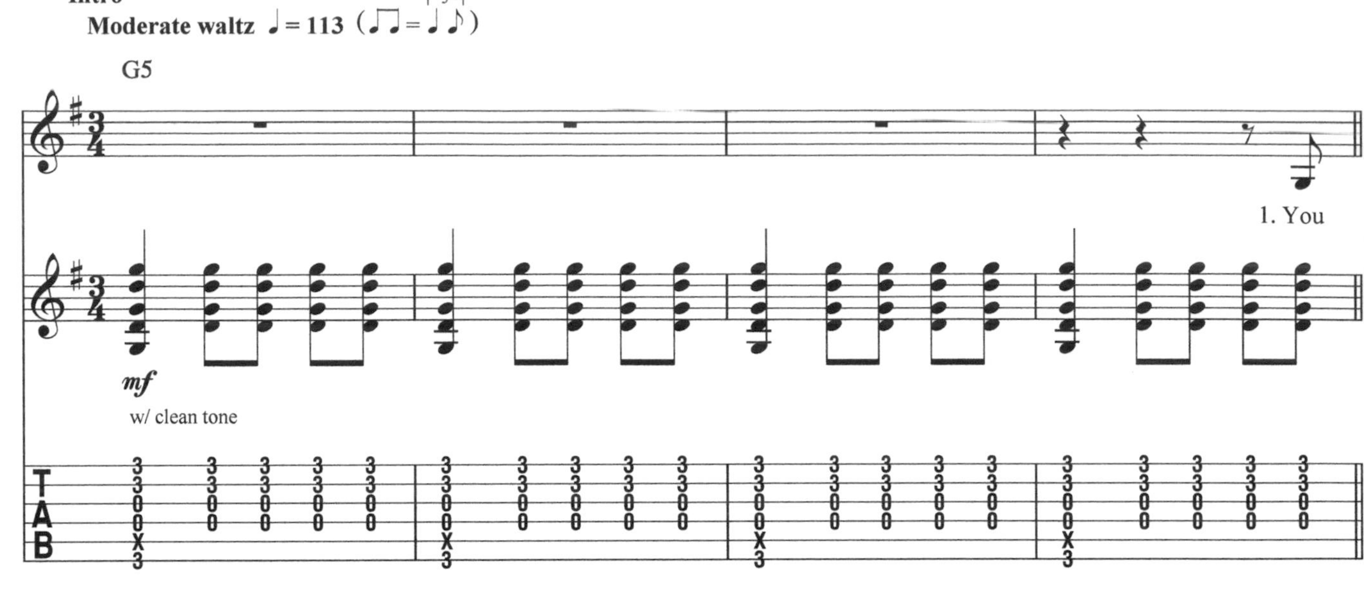
Intro
Moderate waltz ♩ = 113
G5
1. You
mf
w/ clean tone

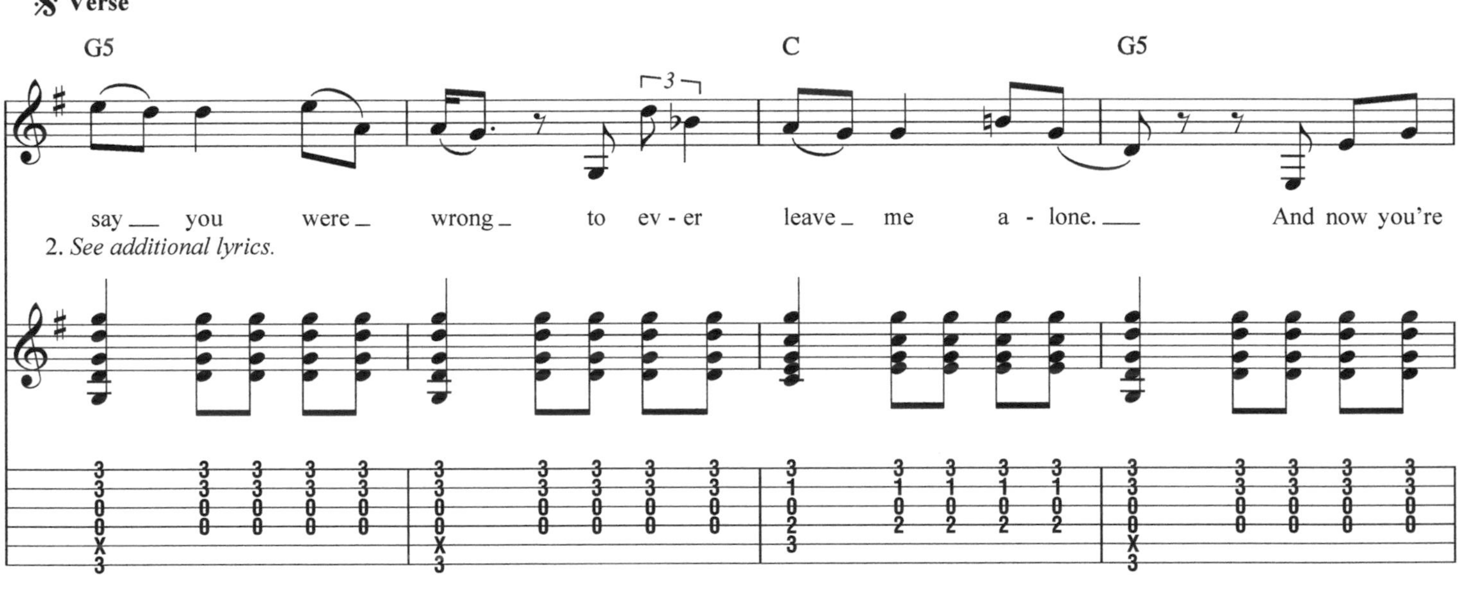
Verse
G5
C
G5
say you were wrong to ev - er leave me a - lone. And now you're
2. See additional lyrics.

D
sor - ry, you're lone - some and scared. And you

G5
C
G5
say you'd be happy if you could just come back home. Well, here's a
quar - ter. Call some - one who cares. Call
D
G5
G7
Chorus
C
G5
some-one who'll lis-ten and might give a damn; may-be
one of your sor - did af - fairs. But don't you
D

G5
G7
C
G5
come a - round here hand - ing me none of your lines. Here's a
To Coda
D
G5
quar - ter. Call some - one who cares.
w/ pick and fingers
Guitar Solo
G5
C7
G
let ring
D
G
C
G

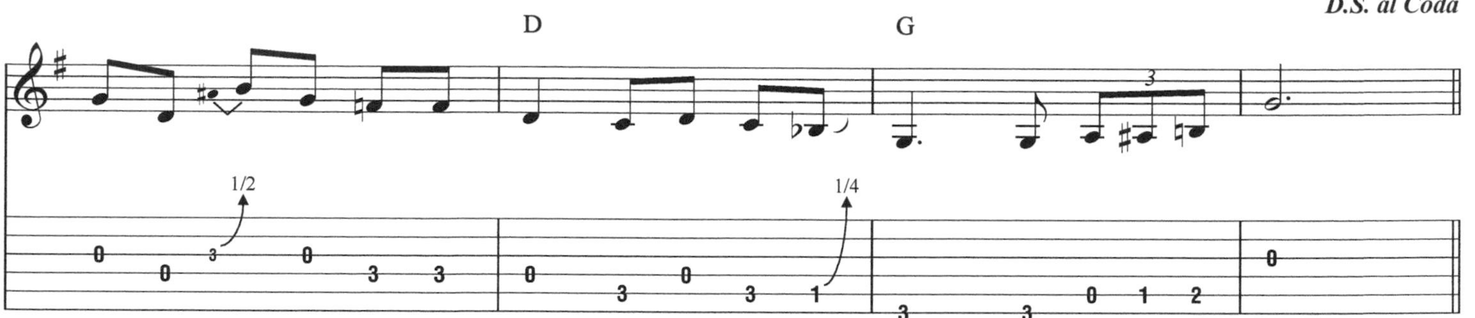

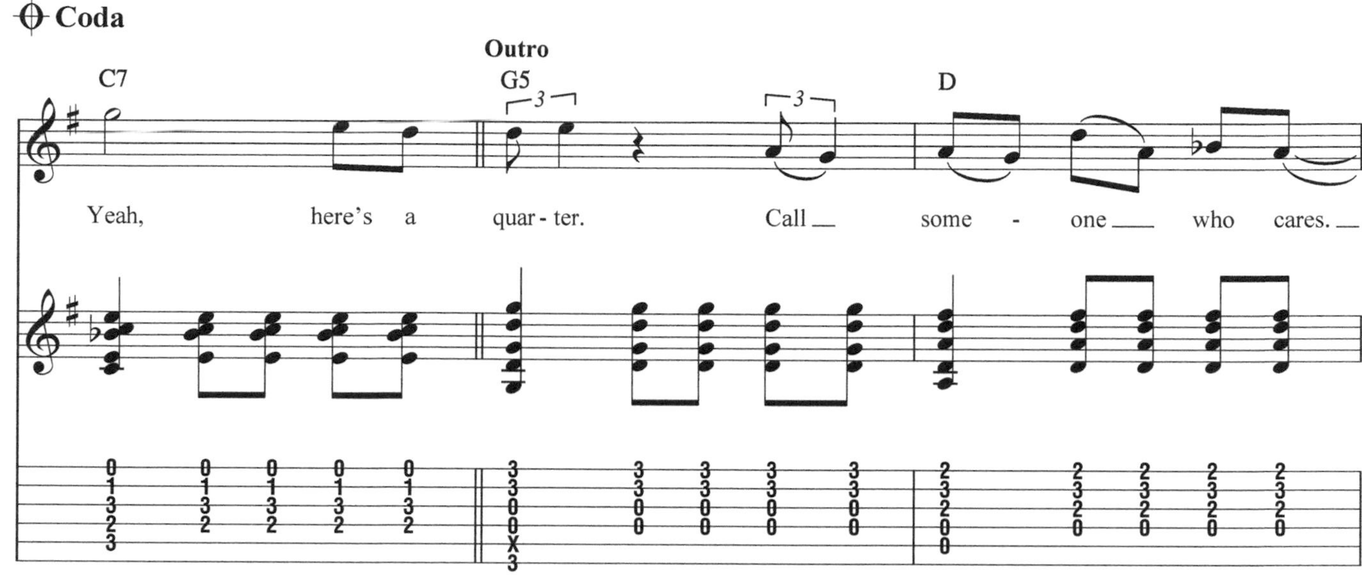

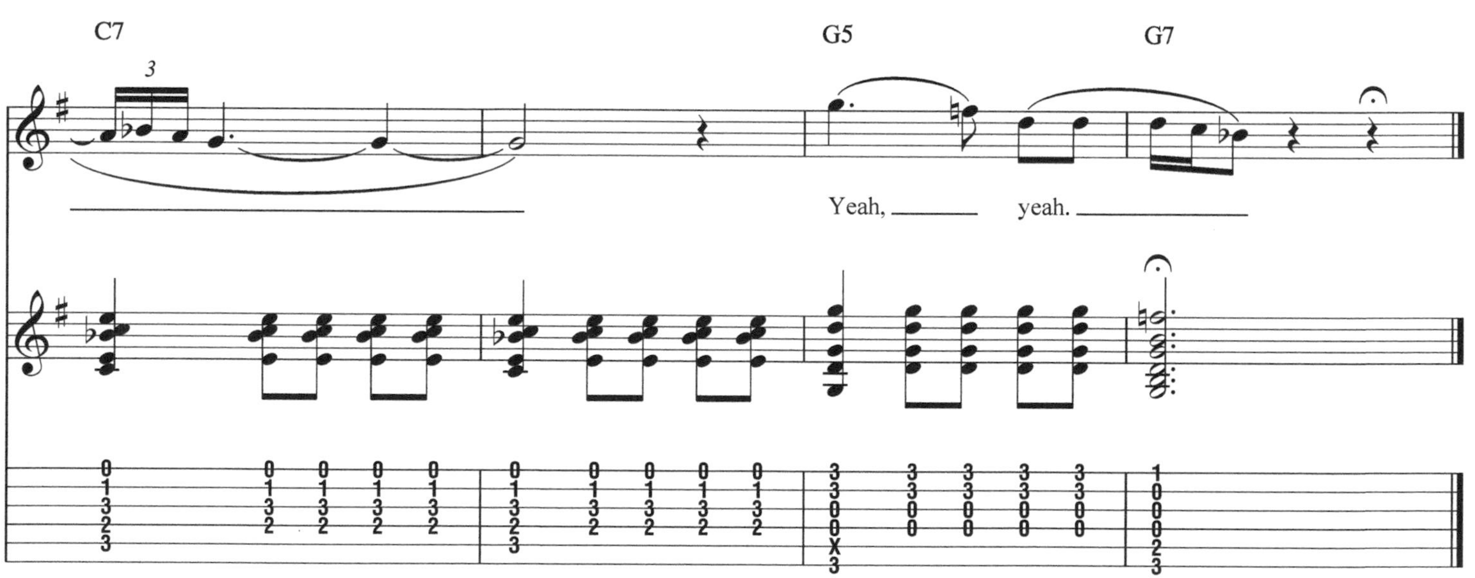

Additional Lyrics

2. Girl, I thought what we had
Could never turn bad,
So your leaving caught me unaware.
But the fact is you've run.
Girl, that can't be undone.
So, here's a quarter.
Call someone who cares.

Mercury Blues

Written by K.C. Douglas and Robert Geddins

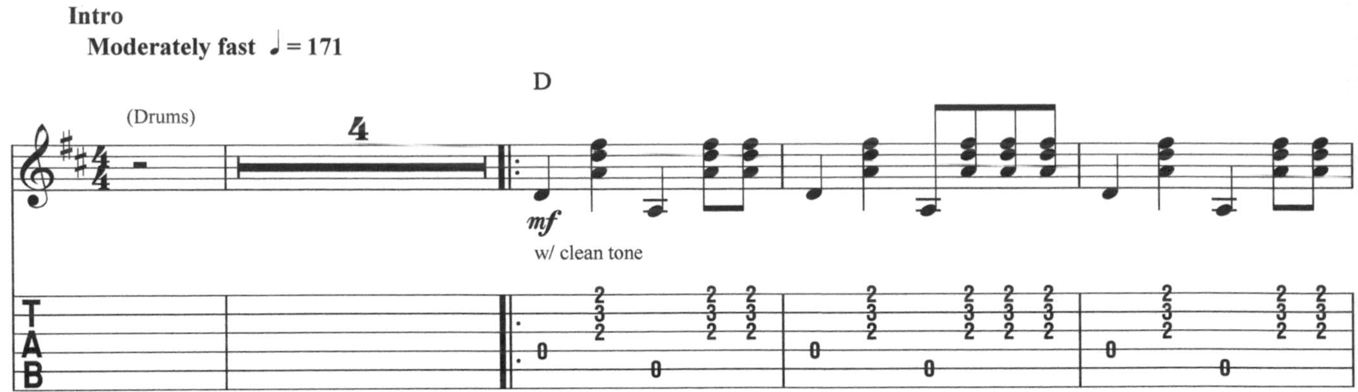

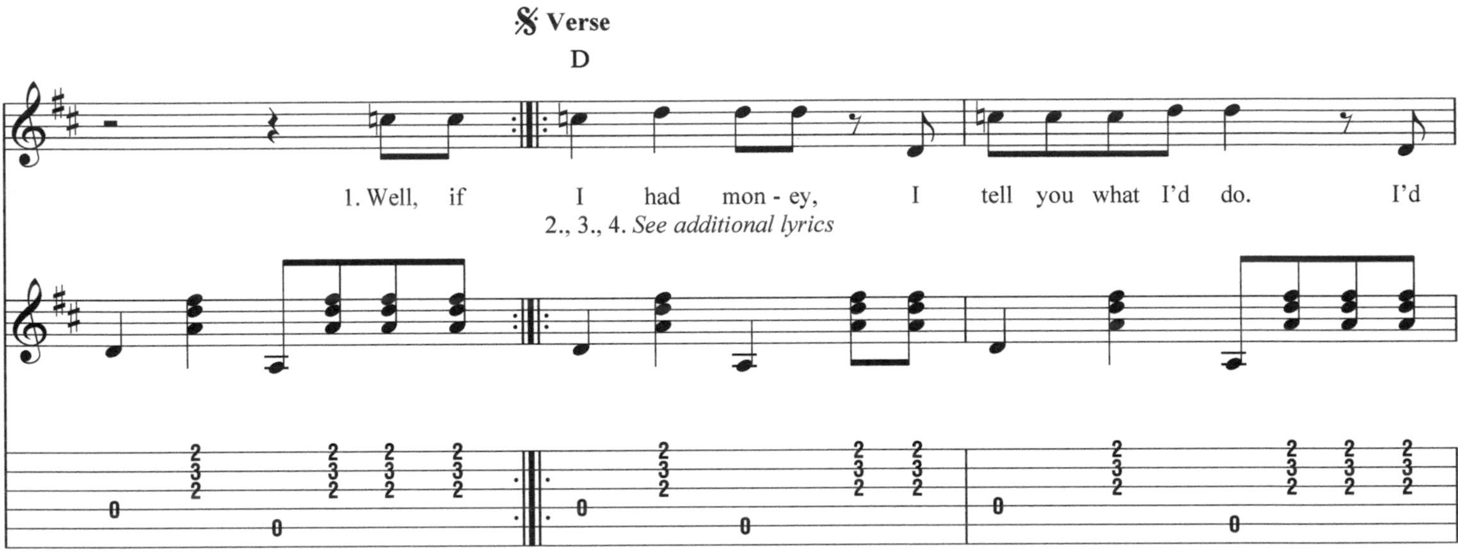

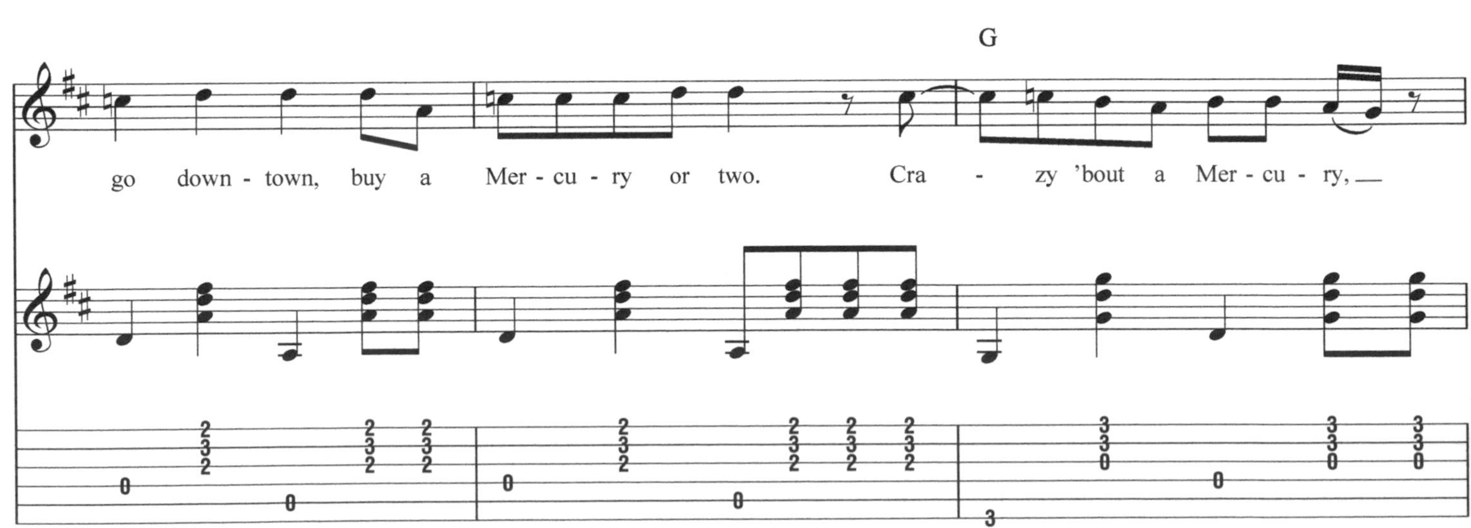

G
D
Lord, I'm cra - zy 'bout a Mer - cu - ry.
I'm gon - na
Bm
A
To Coda 1
1.
D
buy me a Mer - cu - ry and cruise it up and down the road.
To Coda 2
2.
D
Aw, let's go!
w/ thumb pick & fingers
Guitar Solo
D
grad. bend
1/2
1/2

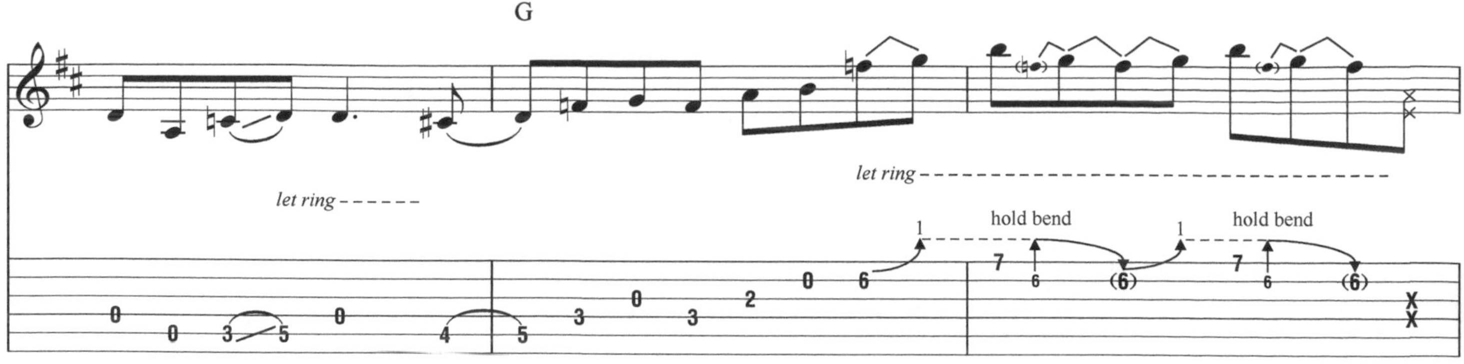
G
let ring
let ring
1
hold bend
1
hold bend

D
Bm
let ring
1/4

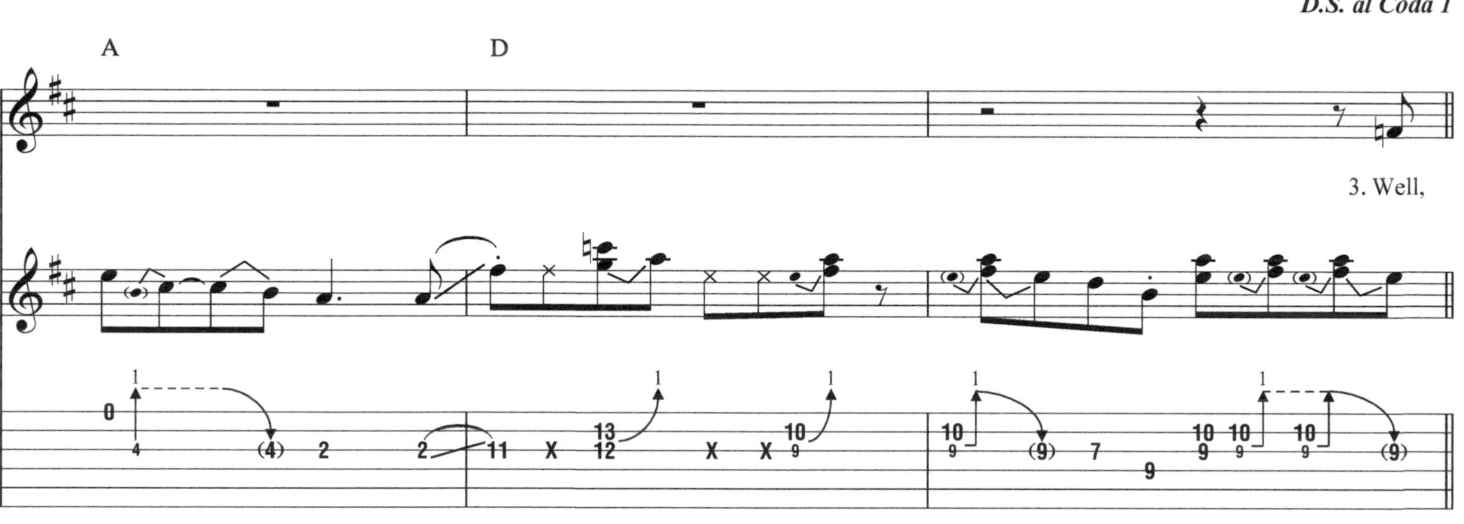
D.S. al Coda 1
A
D
3. Well,

Coda 1
D
Fiddle Solo
D
Spoken: Aw, put it in high gear, now.

G
D
Bm
A
D
D.S. al Coda 2
(take 1st ending)
4. Well, my
Coda 2
Piano Solo
D
G
D

Bm
A
D
5. Well, if
Verse
D N.C.
D N.C.
I had mon-ey, I tell you what I'd do: I'd go down-town, buy a Mer-cu-ry or two. Cra-
G
D
-zy 'bout a Mer-cu-ry, Lord, I'm cra-zy 'bout a Mer-cu-ry. I'm gon-na
Bm
A
G
buy me a Mer-cu-ry and cruise it up and down the road.

Bm
A
I'm gon - na buy me a Mer - cu - ry and cruise it up and down the road.
G
Bm
Yeah, I'm gon - na buy me a Mer - cu - ry and
A
D
cruise it up and down the road.
Aw,
Dobro Solo
D
let's go!

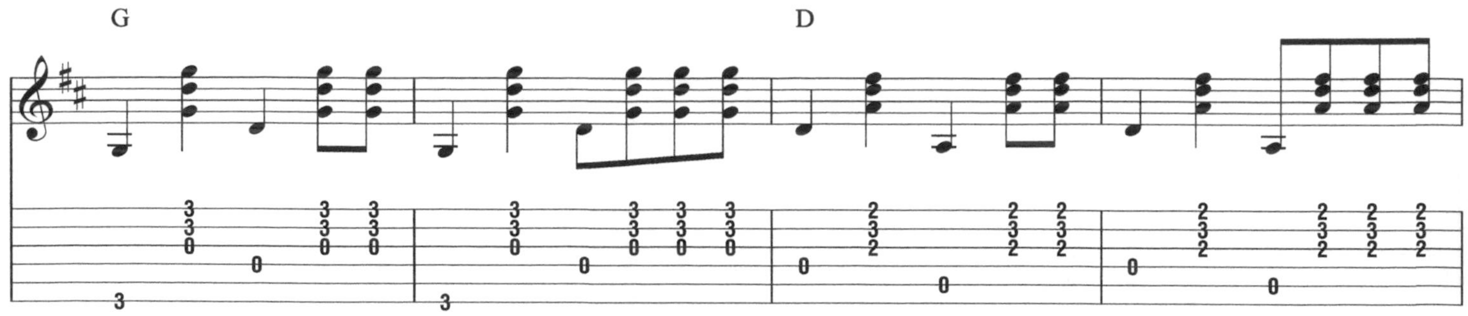

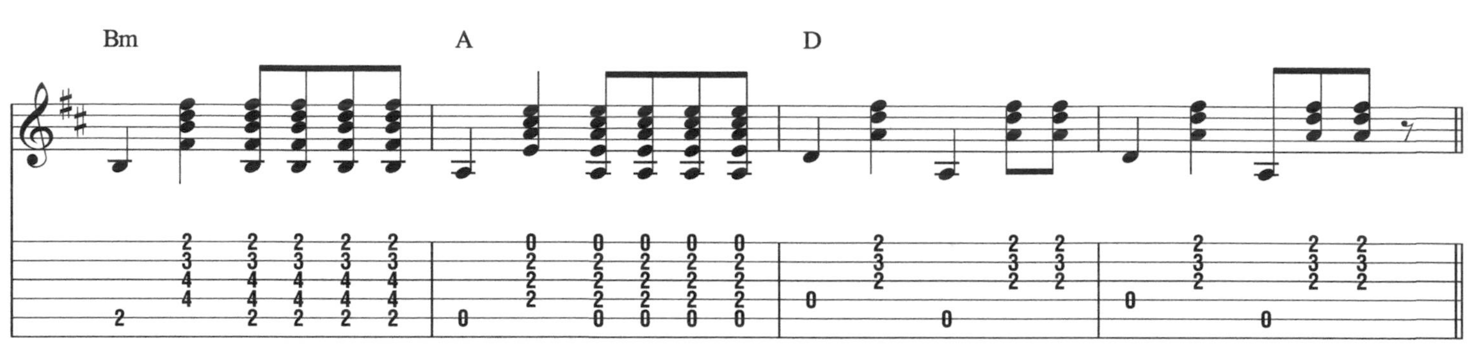

Outro-Guitar Solo

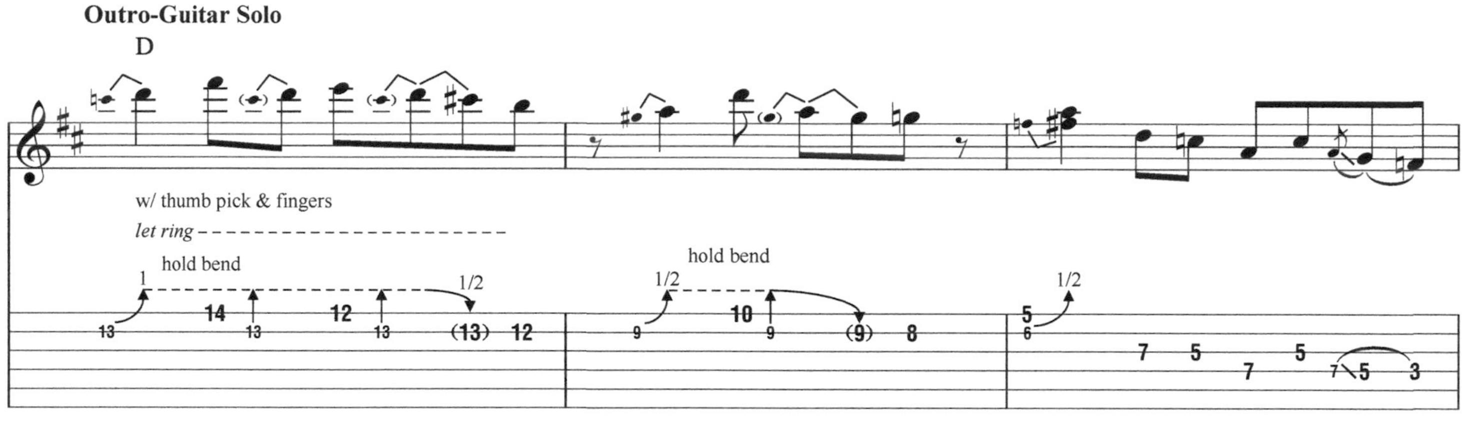

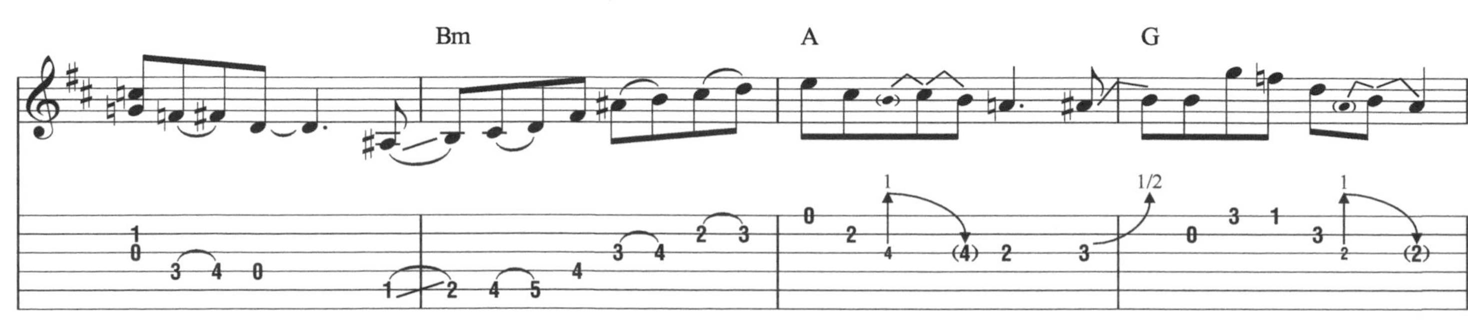

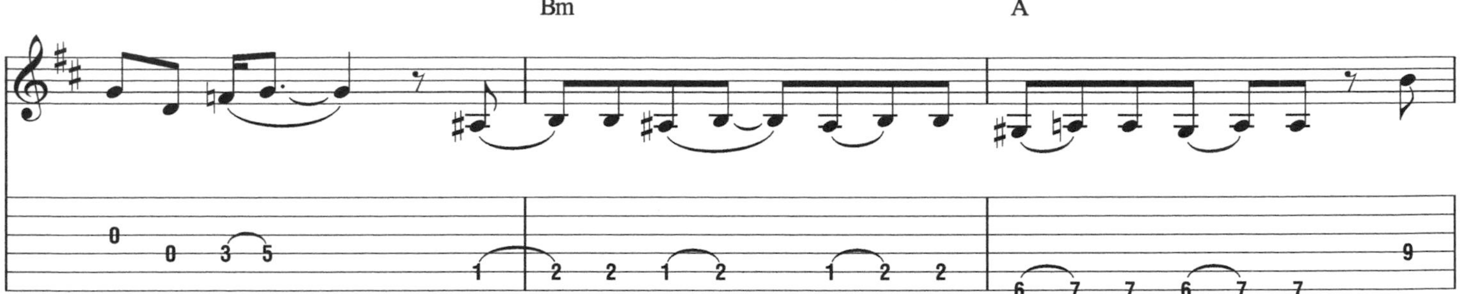

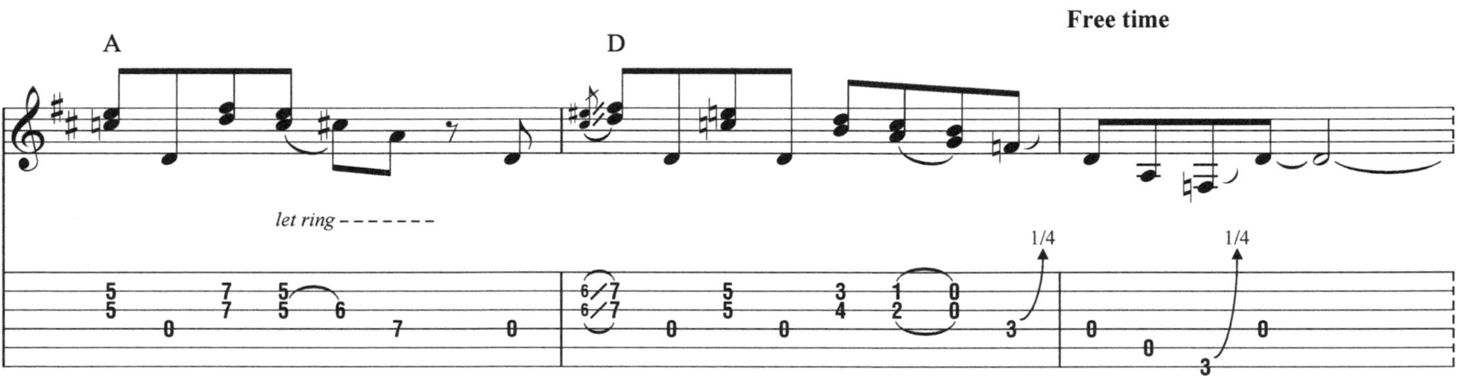

Additional Lyrics

2. Well, the girl I love,
   I stole her from a friend.
   He got lucky, stole her back again.
   She heard he had a Mercury,
   Lord, she's crazy 'bout a Mercury.
   I'm gonna buy me a Mercury
   And cruise it up and down the road.
   Aw, let's go!

3. Well, hey now, mama,
   You look so fine
   Ridin' 'round in your Mercury forty-nine.
   Crazy 'bout a Mercury,
   Lord, I'm crazy 'bout a Mercury.
   I'm gonna buy me a Mercury
   And cruise it up and down the road.
   Aw, put it in high gear now.

4. Well, my baby went out,
   She didn't stay long.
   Bought herself a Mercury, come a cruisin' home.
   She's crazy 'bout a Mercury,
   Yeah, she's crazy 'bout a Mercury.
   I'm gonna buy me a Mercury
   And cruise it up and down the road.
   Aw, cruise now.

One More Last Chance

Words and Music by Gary Nicholson and Vince Gill

Drop D tuning:
(low to high) D-A-D-G-B-E

Intro
Moderately fast ♩ = 177

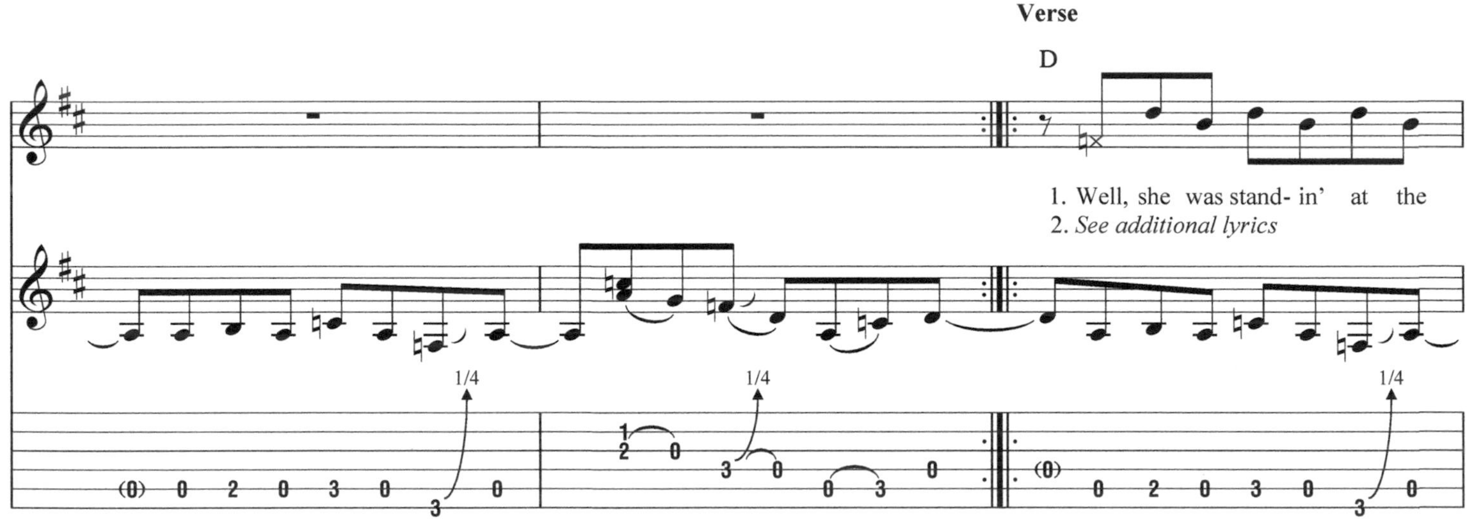

A
good book in her left hand and a roll-ing pin in her right.
1/4
1/2
1/4
1/4
D
She said, "You've come home for the last time with a
1/4
1/4
G
D
whis - key on your breath.
If you don't lis - ten to my
1/4
1/4
1/4
1/4
A
D
preach-in', boy, I'm gon - na have to beat you half to death."
1/2
1/4
1/4

Chorus
3rd time, substitute Fill 1
D
Give me just a one more last chance be-
G
D
fore you say we're through. I know I drive you cra-
A
-zy, ba-by; it's the best that I can do. We're just some
D
G
good old boys mak-in' noise. I ain't a run-ning a-round on
Fill 1

D
G
D
you. Give me just a one more last chance be -
1/4
1/2
grad. bend
1.
To Coda
A
D
fore you say we're through.
2.
2. Well, fore you say we're through.
Guitar Solo

G
D
1
1/4

A
1
1/2
1
1
1
hold bend

D
1/4
1/4
1/2
1/2

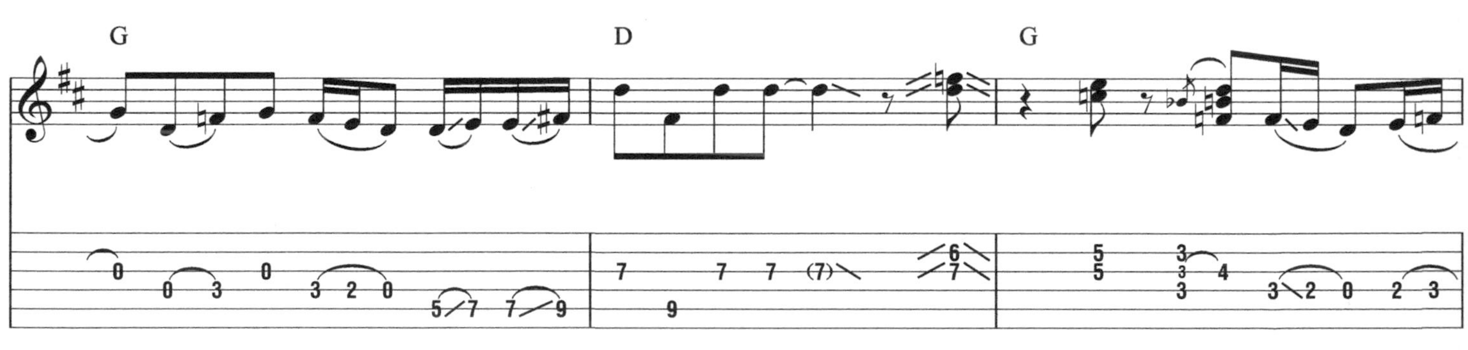
G
D
G

D
A
D
1
1

Additional Lyrics

2. Well, first she hid my glasses because she knows that I can't see.
She said, "You ain't goin' nowhere, boy, 'til you spend a little time with me."
Well, then the boys called from the honky-tonk, said there's a party goin' on down here.
Well, she might have took my car keys, but she forgot about my old John Deere.

Mountain Music

Words and Music by Randy Owen

Then I'll float on down the riv - er to a Ca -

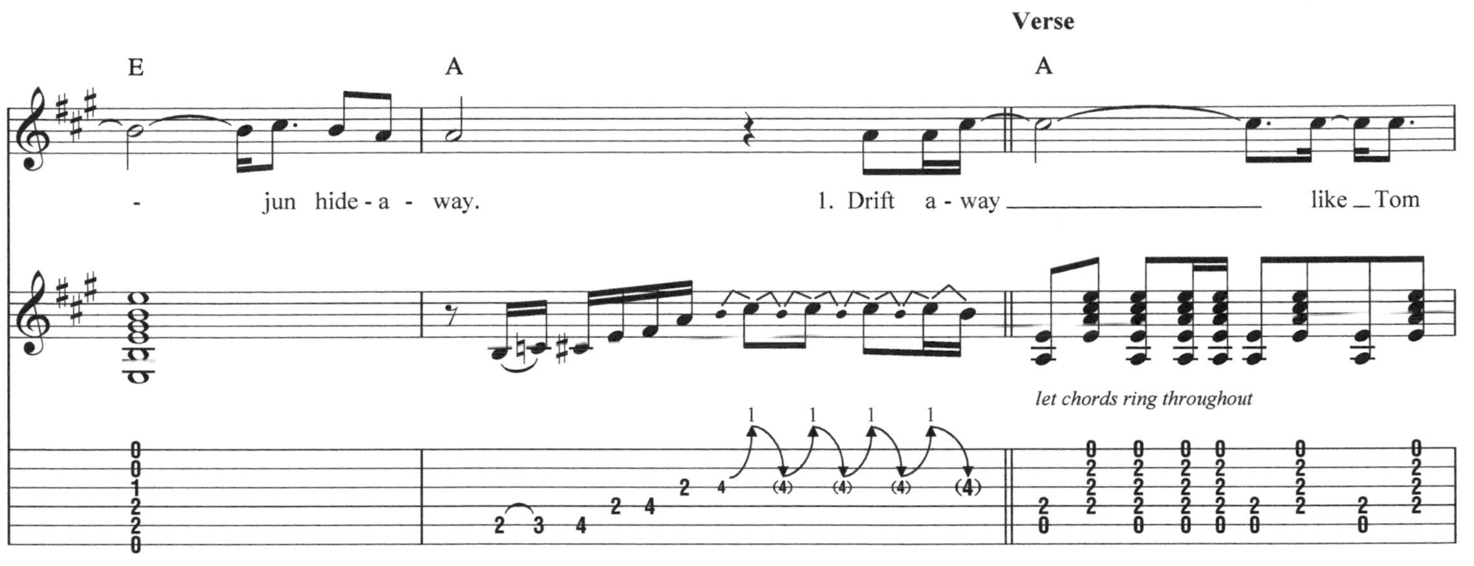
Verse
E
A
A
- jun hide - a - way.
1. Drift a - way like Tom
let chords ring throughout

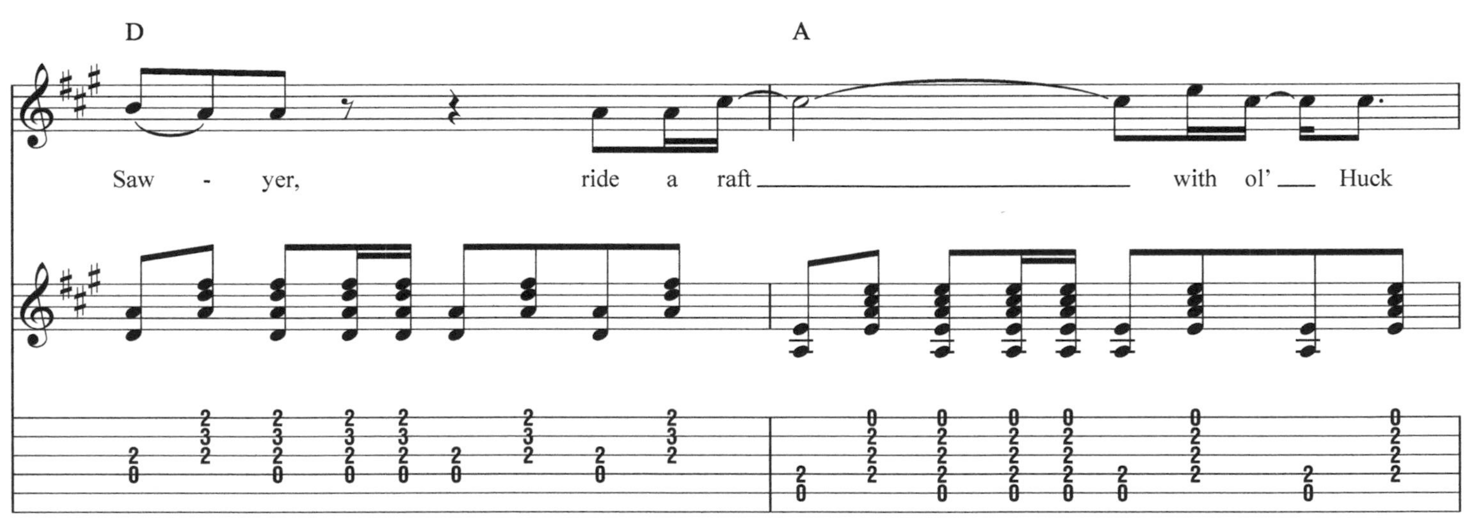
D
A
Saw - yer, ride a raft with ol' Huck

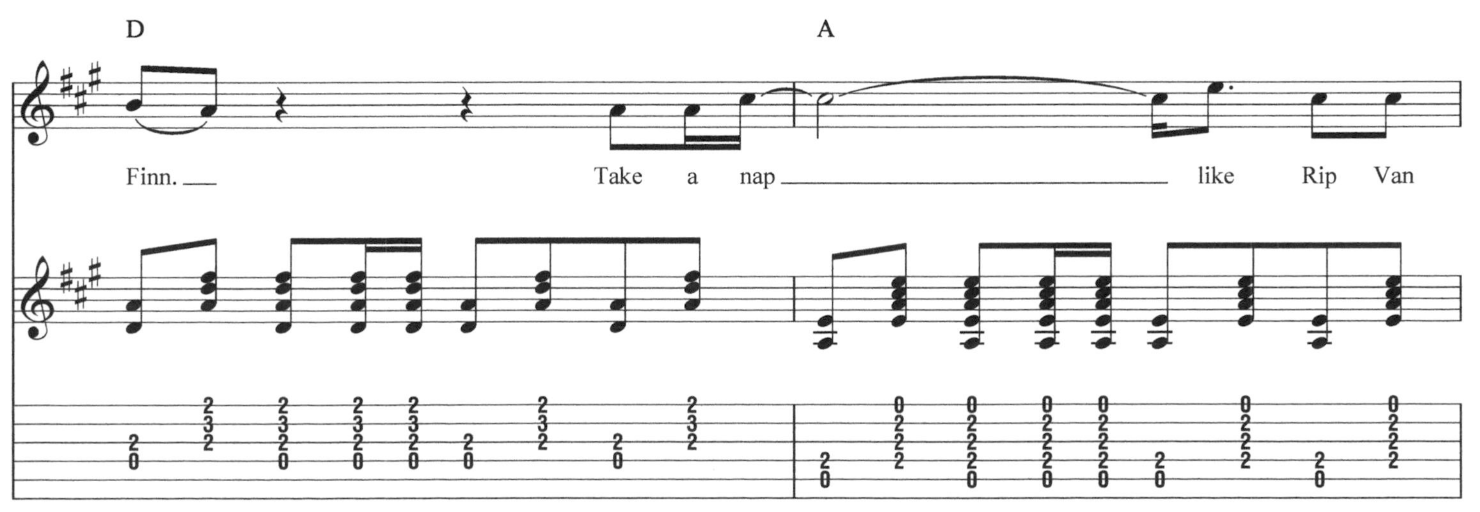
D
A
Finn. Take a nap like Rip Van

D
G
Win - kle, daze dream - in' a -
E
Chorus
A
gain. Oh, play me some moun - tain
D
A
mu - sic, like grand - ma and grand - pa used to play.
D
A
Then I'll float on down the riv -

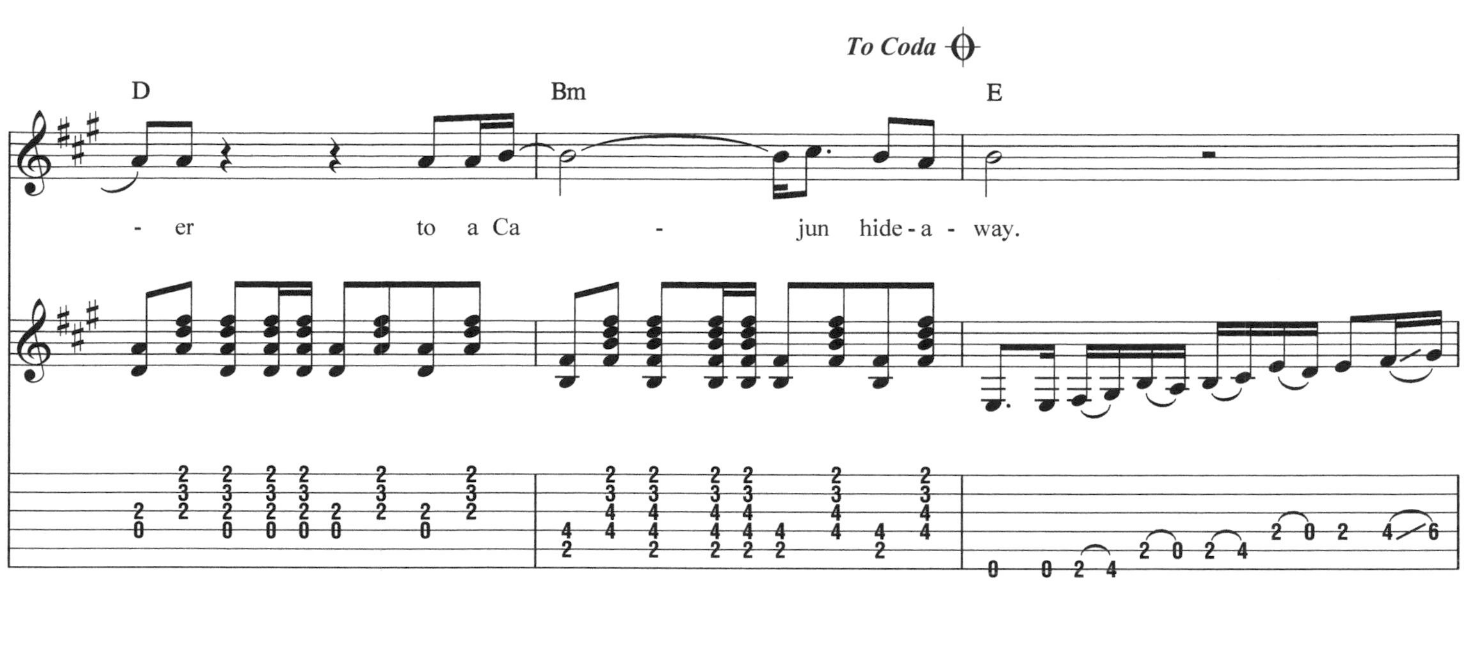
To Coda
D
Bm
E
- er to a Ca - jun hide - a - way.

Guitar Solo
C#m
D
A
C#m
hold bend
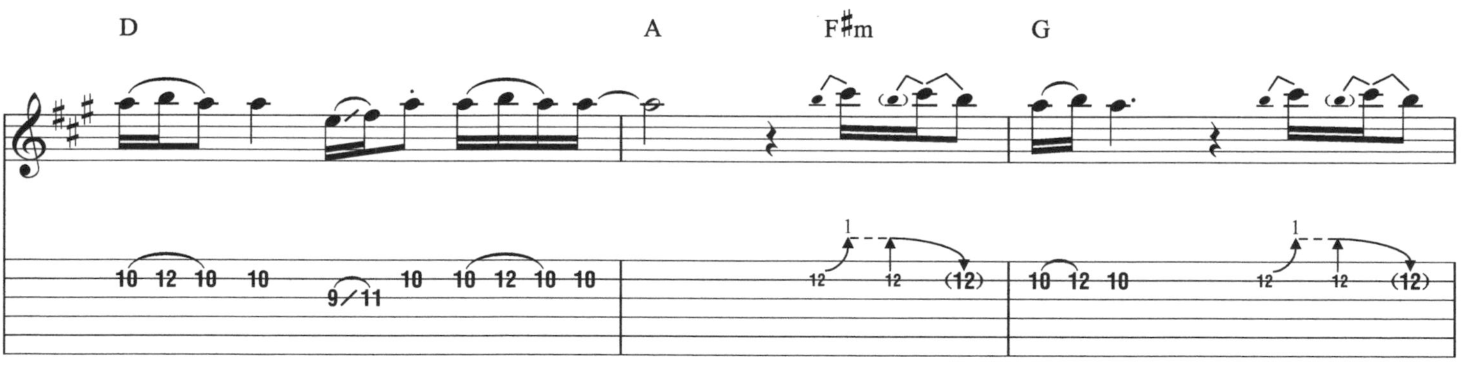
D
A
F#m
G
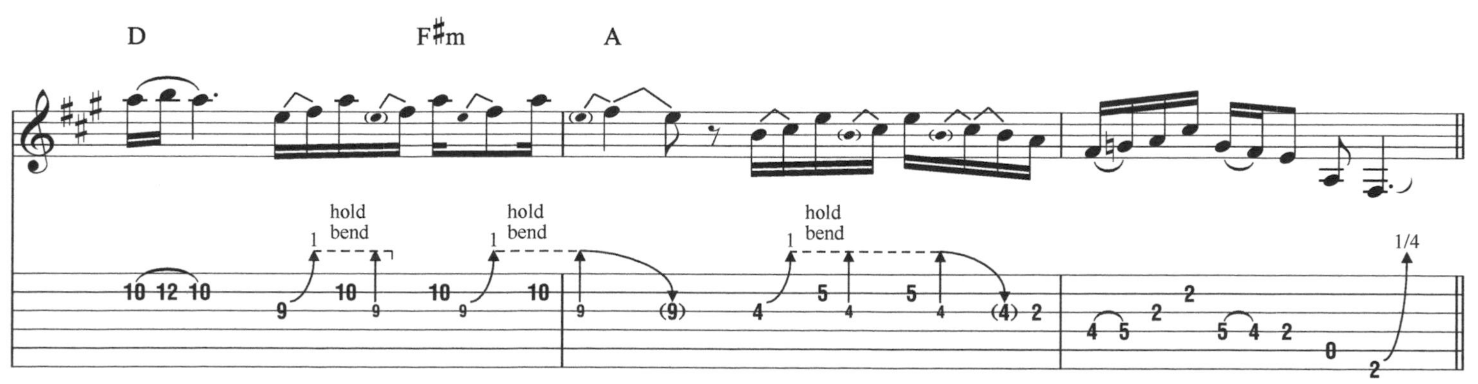
D
F#m
A
hold bend
hold bend
hold bend
1/4

Verse

A
D
2. Swim a - cross the riv - er just to prove
3. See additional lyrics
that I'm a man. Spend the day
be - in' la - zy, just
1.
G
E
be - in' na - ture's friend.

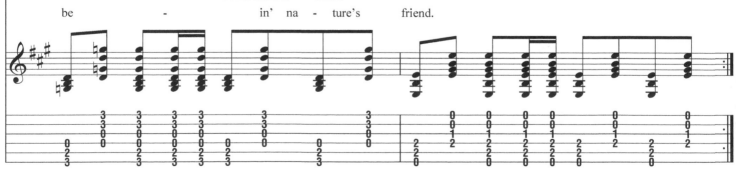

2.
E
bats.
Play some
Bridge
N.C.(A)
back-home, come-on mu - sic that comes from the heart.
Play some-thing with lots of feel - in', 'cause that's where
D.S. al Coda
Bm
E
mu - sic has to start.
Oh,

Coda

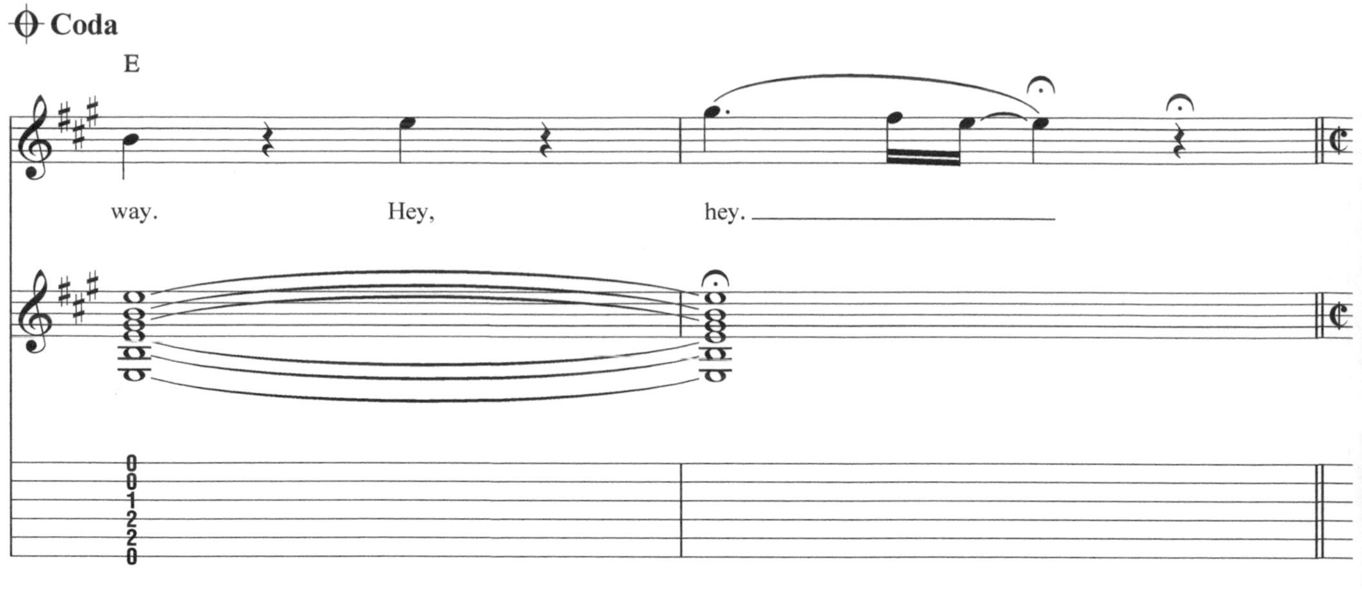

Interlude

Faster 𝅗𝅥 = 75

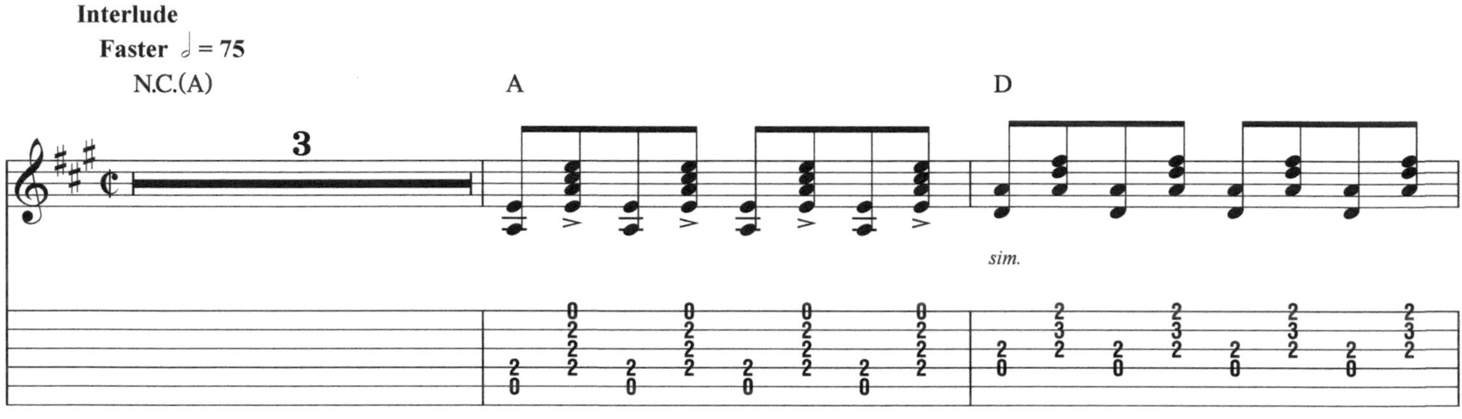

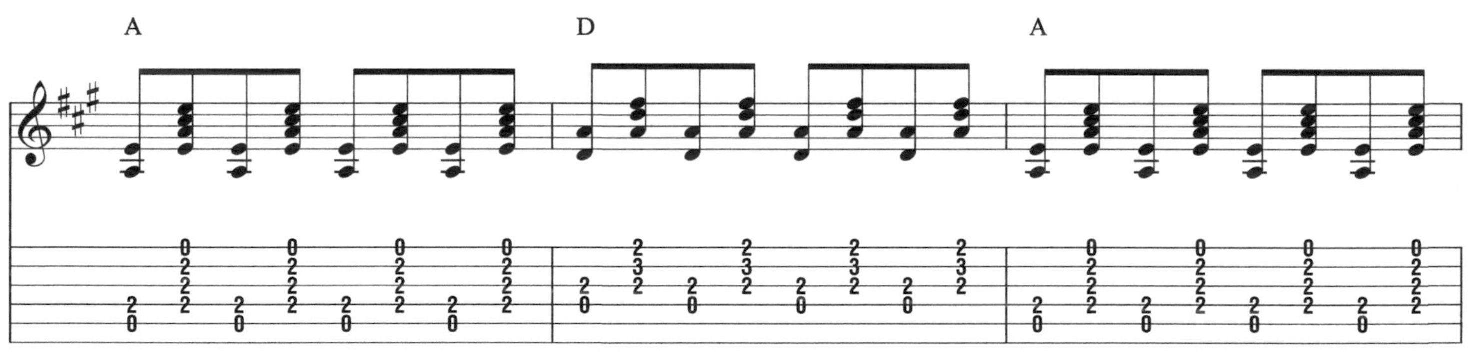

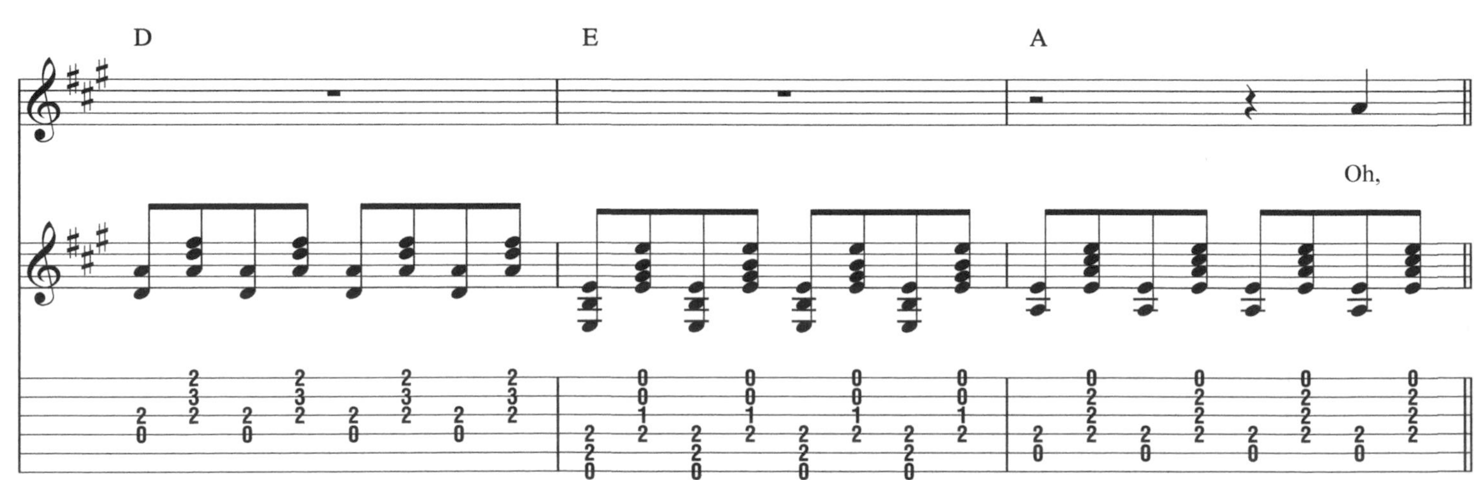

Chorus
A
D
play me moun - tain mu - sic. Oh,
A
D
play me moun - tain mu - sic. Oh,
A
D
play me moun - tain mu - sic. Oh,
E
A
play.

Outro

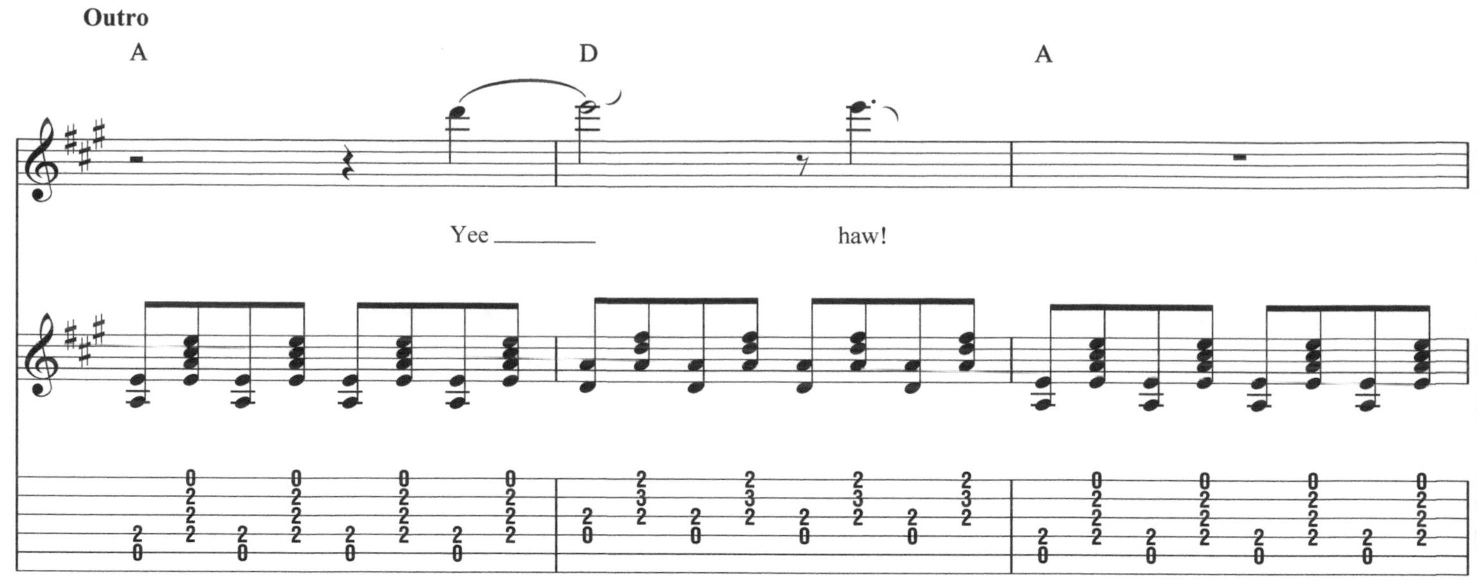

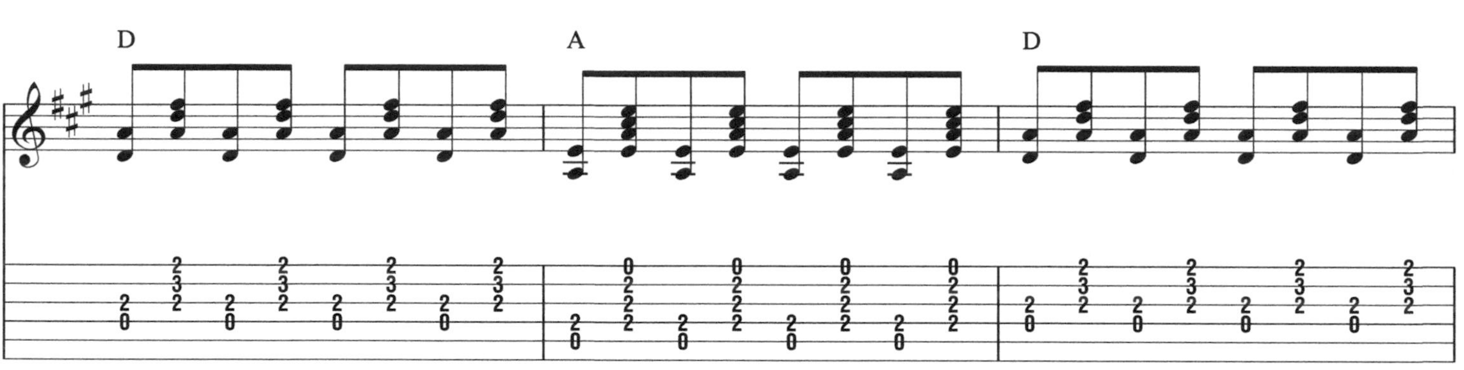

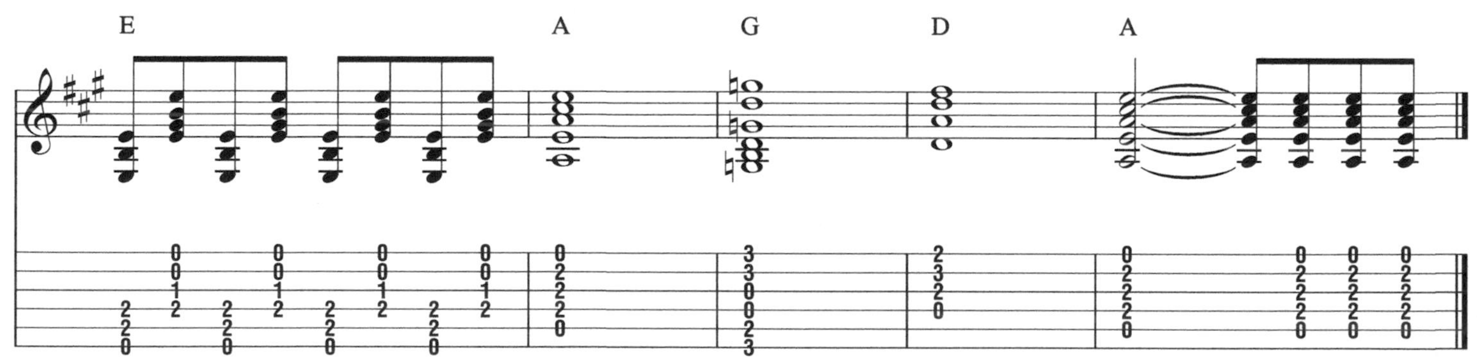

Additional Lyrics

2. Climb a long tall hick'ry,
 Bend it over, "Skinnin' cats."
 Playin' baseball with chert rocks,
 Usin' saw mill slabs for bats.

The Only Daddy That Will Walk the Line

Words and Music by Ivy J. Bryant

Tune down 1/2 step:
(low to high) Eb-Ab-Db-Gb-Bb-Eb

Intro
Moderately ♩ = 161
E7
mf
w/ clean tone
w/ pick & fingers

Verse
E
1. Ev - 'ry - bod - y knows you been step - pin' on my toes and I'm get - tin' pret - ty tired of it.
2., 3. See additional lyrics

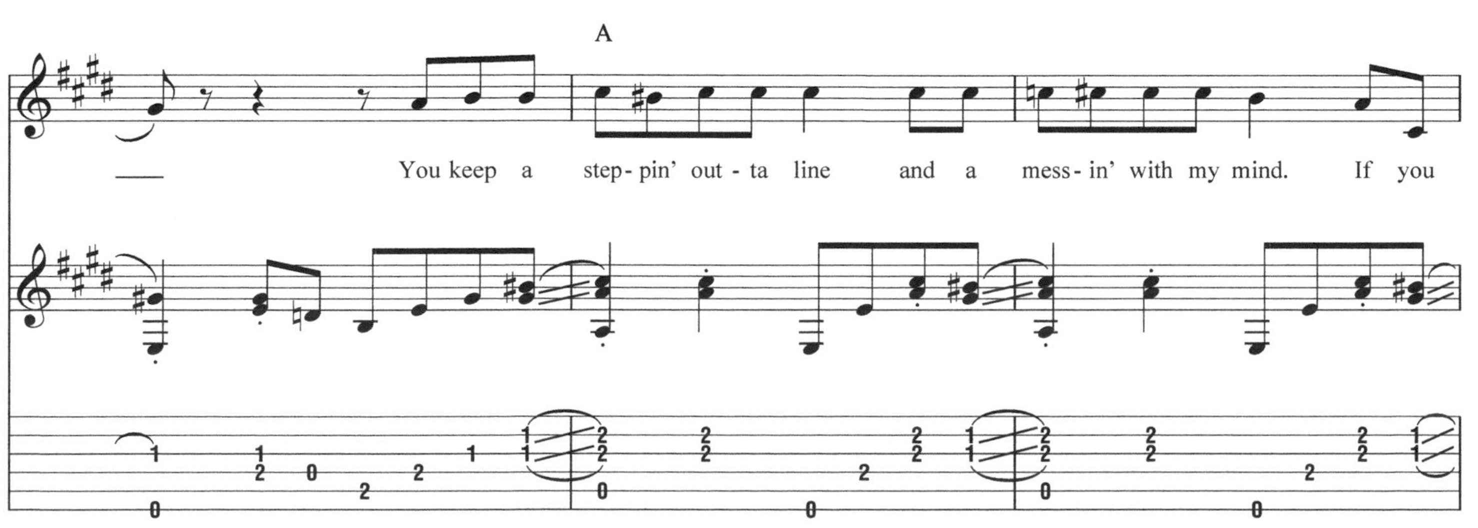
A
You keep a step - pin' out - ta line and a mess - in' with my mind. If you

B7
had an - y sense, you'd quit, 'cause ev - er since you were a lit - tle
bit - ty teen - y girl, you said I was the on - ly man in this whole world. And
E
now you bet - ter do some think - in', then you'll find you got the on -
To Coda
E7
- ly dad - dy that - 'll walk the line.

1.
2. I keep ah,
2.
Guitar Solo
E
1/2
A
1
B7
let ring
hold bend

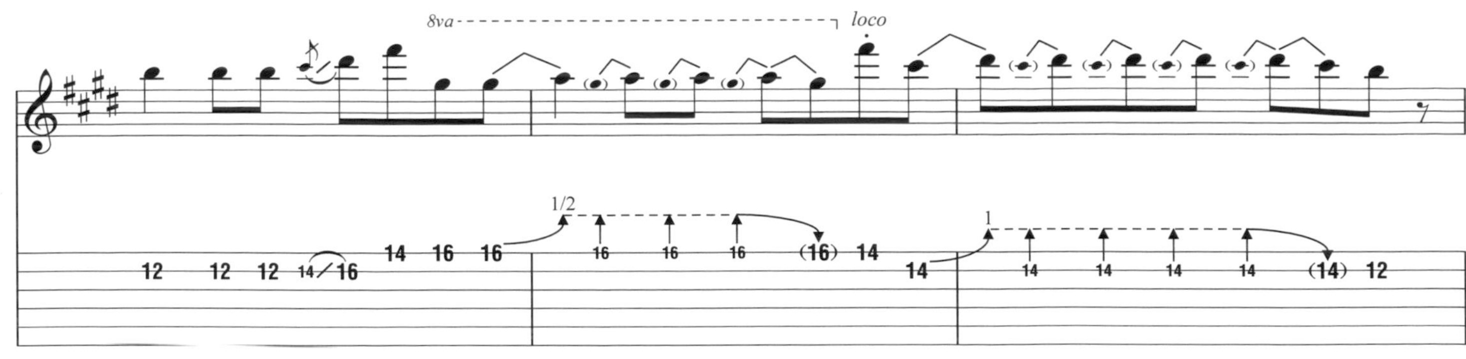

8va
loco
1/2
1

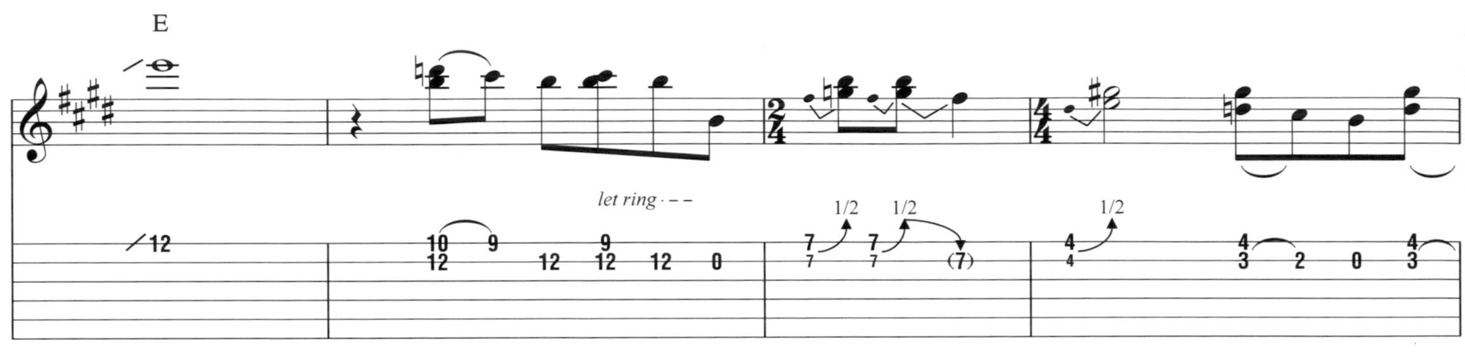

E
let ring
1/2

D.S. al Coda
3. You keep a
1/2

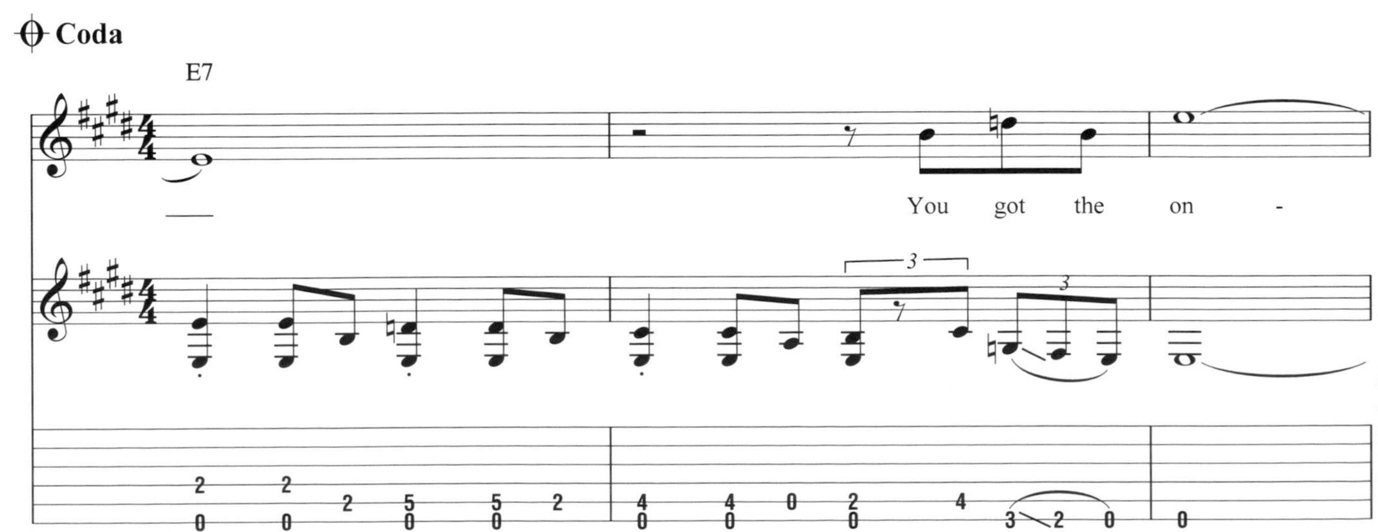

Coda
E7
You got the on -

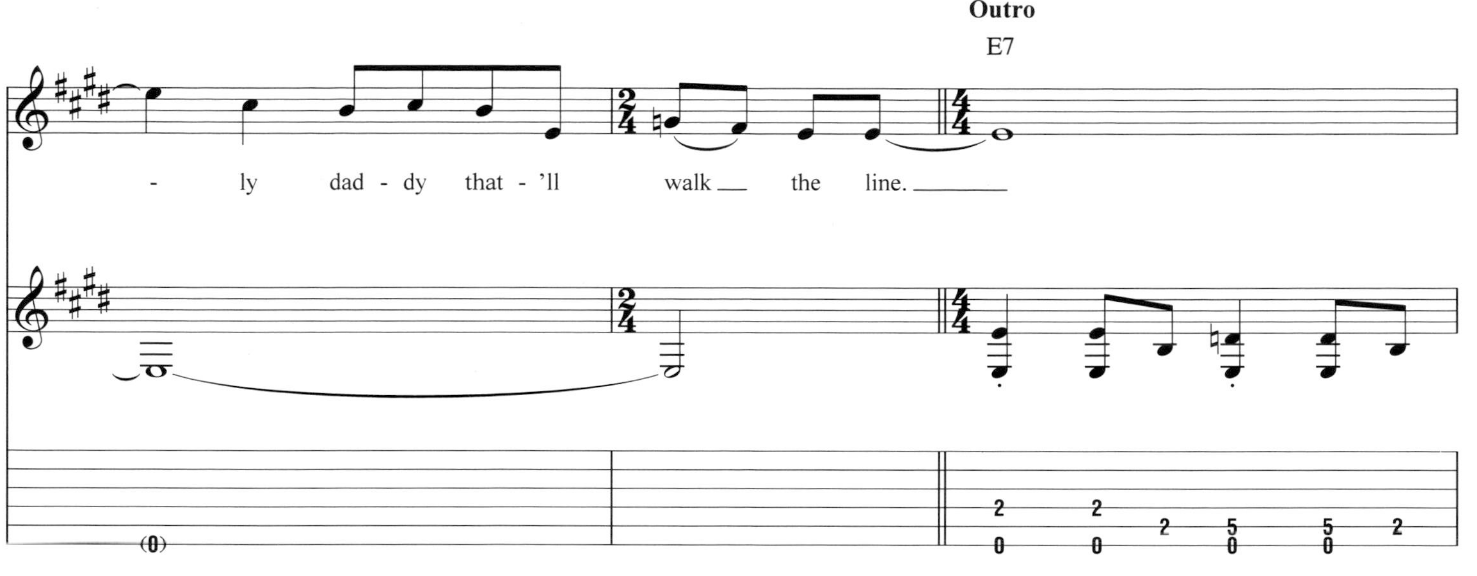

Additional Lyrics

2. I keep a workin' ev'ry day, all you wanna do is play.
   I'm tired of stayin' out all night.
   I'm a comin' unglued from your funny little moods.
   Now honey, baby, that ain't right,
   'Cause ever since you were a little bitty teeny girl,
   You said I was the only man in this whole world.
   And now you better do some thinkin',
   Then you'll find you got the only daddy that'll walk the line.

3. You keep a packin' up my clothes,
   Nearly ev'rybody knows that you're still just a puttin' me on.
   But when I start a walkin', gonna hear you start a squawkin'
   And a beggin' me to come back home,
   'Cause ever since you were a little bitty teeny girl,
   You said I was the only man in this whole world.
   And now you better do some thinkin',
   Then you'll find you got the only daddy that'll walk the line.
   You got the only daddy that'll walk the line.

HAL•LEONARD® GUITAR PLAY-ALONG

Complete song lists available online.

This series will help you play your favorite songs quickly and easily. Just follow the tab and listen to the audio to the hear how the guitar should sound, and then play along using the separate backing tracks. Audio files also include software to slow down the tempo without changing pitch. The melody and lyrics are included in the book so that you can sing or simply follow along.

INCLUDES TAB

VOL. 1 – ROCK ... 00699570 / $17.99
VOL. 2 – ACOUSTIC ... 00699569 / $16.99
VOL. 3 – HARD ROCK ... 00699573 / $17.99
VOL. 4 – POP/ROCK ... 00699571 / $16.99
VOL. 5 – THREE CHORD SONGS ... 00300985 / $16.99
VOL. 6 – '90S ROCK ... 00298615 / $16.99
VOL. 7 – BLUES ... 00699575 / $19.99
VOL. 8 – ROCK ... 00699585 / $16.99
VOL. 9 – EASY ACOUSTIC SONGS ... 00151708 / $16.99
VOL. 10 – ACOUSTIC ... 00699586 / $16.95
VOL. 11 – EARLY ROCK ... 00699579 / $15.99
VOL. 12 – ROCK POP ... 00291724 / $17.99
VOL. 14 – BLUES ROCK ... 00699582 / $16.99
VOL. 15 – R&B ... 00699583 / $17.99
VOL. 16 – JAZZ ... 00699584 / $16.99
VOL. 17 – COUNTRY ... 00699588 / $17.99
VOL. 18 – ACOUSTIC ROCK ... 00699577 / $15.95
VOL. 20 – ROCKABILLY ... 00699580 / $17.99
VOL. 21 – SANTANA ... 00174525 / $17.99
VOL. 22 – CHRISTMAS ... 00699600 / $15.99
VOL. 23 – SURF ... 00699635 / $17.99
VOL. 24 – ERIC CLAPTON ... 00699649 / $19.99
VOL. 25 – THE BEATLES ... 00198265 / $19.99
VOL. 26 – ELVIS PRESLEY ... 00699643 / $16.99
VOL. 27 – DAVID LEE ROTH ... 00699645 / $16.95
VOL. 28 – GREG KOCH ... 00699646 / $19.99
VOL. 29 – BOB SEGER ... 00699647 / $16.99
VOL. 30 – KISS ... 00699644 / $17.99
VOL. 32 – THE OFFSPRING ... 00699653 / $14.95
VOL. 33 – ACOUSTIC CLASSICS ... 00699656 / $19.99
VOL. 35 – HAIR METAL ... 00699660 / $17.99
VOL. 36 – SOUTHERN ROCK ... 00699661 / $19.99
VOL. 37 – ACOUSTIC UNPLUGGED ... 00699662 / $22.99
VOL. 38 – BLUES ... 00699663 / $17.99
VOL. 39 – '80s METAL ... 00699664 / $17.99
VOL. 40 – INCUBUS ... 00699668 / $17.95
VOL. 41 – ERIC CLAPTON ... 00699669 / $17.99
VOL. 42 – COVER BAND HITS ... 00211597 / $16.99
VOL. 43 – LYNYRD SKYNYRD ... 00699681 / $22.99
VOL. 44 – JAZZ GREATS ... 00699689 / $19.99
VOL. 45 – TV THEMES ... 00699718 / $14.95
VOL. 46 – MAINSTREAM ROCK ... 00699722 / $16.95
VOL. 47 – JIMI HENDRIX SMASH HITS ... 00699723 / $22.99
VOL. 48 – AEROSMITH CLASSICS ... 00699724 / $19.99
VOL. 49 – STEVIE RAY VAUGHAN ... 00699725 / $17.99
VOL. 50 – VAN HALEN: 1978-1984 ... 00110269 / $19.99
VOL. 51 – ALTERNATIVE '90s ... 00699727 / $14.99
VOL. 52 – FUNK ... 00699728 / $15.99
VOL. 53 – DISCO ... 00699729 / $14.99
VOL. 54 – HEAVY METAL ... 00699730 / $17.99
VOL. 55 – POP METAL ... 00699731 / $14.95
VOL. 57 – GUNS 'N' ROSES ... 00159922 / $19.99
VOL. 58 – BLINK 182 ... 00699772 / $17.99
VOL. 59 – CHET ATKINS ... 00702347 / $17.99
VOL. 60 – 3 DOORS DOWN ... 00699774 / $14.95
VOL. 62 – CHRISTMAS CAROLS ... 00699798 / $12.95
VOL. 63 – CREEDENCE CLEARWATER REVIVAL ... 00699802 / $17.99
VOL. 64 – ULTIMATE OZZY OSBOURNE ... 00699803 / $19.99
VOL. 66 – THE ROLLING STONES ... 00699807 / $19.99
VOL. 67 – BLACK SABBATH ... 00699808 / $17.99
VOL. 68 – PINK FLOYD – DARK SIDE OF THE MOON ... 00699809 / $17.99
VOL. 71 – CHRISTIAN ROCK ... 00699824 / $14.95
VOL. 74 – SIMPLE STRUMMING SONGS ... 00151706 / $19.99
VOL. 75 – TOM PETTY ... 00699882 / $19.99
VOL. 76 – COUNTRY HITS ... 00699884 / $16.99
VOL. 77 – BLUEGRASS ... 00699910 / $17.99
VOL. 78 – NIRVANA ... 00700132 / $17.99
VOL. 79 – NEIL YOUNG ... 00700133 / $24.99
VOL. 81 – ROCK ANTHOLOGY ... 00700176 / $22.99
VOL. 82 – EASY ROCK SONGS ... 00700177 / $17.99
VOL. 83 – SUBLIME ... 00369114 / $17.99
VOL. 84 – STEELY DAN ... 00700200 / $19.99
VOL. 85 – THE POLICE ... 00700269 / $17.99
VOL. 86 – BOSTON ... 00700465 / $19.99
VOL. 87 – ACOUSTIC WOMEN ... 00700763 / $14.99
VOL. 88 – GRUNGE ... 00700467 / $16.99
VOL. 89 – REGGAE ... 00700468 / $15.99
VOL. 90 – CLASSICAL POP ... 00700469 / $14.99
VOL. 91 – BLUES INSTRUMENTALS ... 00700505 / $19.99
VOL. 92 – EARLY ROCK INSTRUMENTALS ... 00700506 / $17.99
VOL. 93 – ROCK INSTRUMENTALS ... 00700507 / $17.99
VOL. 94 – SLOW BLUES ... 00700508 / $16.99
VOL. 95 – BLUES CLASSICS ... 00700509 / $15.99
VOL. 96 – BEST COUNTRY HITS ... 00211615 / $16.99
VOL. 97 – CHRISTMAS CLASSICS ... 00236542 / $14.99
VOL. 99 – ZZ TOP ... 00700762 / $17.99
VOL. 100 – B.B. KING ... 00700466 / $16.99
VOL. 101 – SONGS FOR BEGINNERS ... 00701917 / $14.99
VOL. 102 – CLASSIC PUNK ... 00700769 / $14.99
VOL. 104 – DUANE ALLMAN ... 00700846 / $22.99
VOL. 105 – LATIN ... 00700939 / $16.99
VOL. 106 – WEEZER ... 00700958 / $17.99
VOL. 107 – CREAM ... 00701069 / $17.99
VOL. 108 – THE WHO ... 00701053 / $17.99
VOL. 109 – STEVE MILLER ... 00701054 / $19.99
VOL. 110 – SLIDE GUITAR HITS ... 00701055 / $17.99
VOL. 111 – JOHN MELLENCAMP ... 00701056 / $14.99
VOL. 112 – QUEEN ... 00701052 / $16.99
VOL. 113 – JIM CROCE ... 00701058 / $19.99
VOL. 114 – BON JOVI ... 00701060 / $17.99
VOL. 115 – JOHNNY CASH ... 00701070 / $17.99
VOL. 116 – THE VENTURES ... 00701124 / $17.99
VOL. 117 – BRAD PAISLEY ... 00701224 / $16.99
VOL. 118 – ERIC JOHNSON ... 00701353 / $19.99
VOL. 119 – AC/DC CLASSICS ... 00701356 / $19.99
VOL. 120 – PROGRESSIVE ROCK ... 00701457 / $14.99
VOL. 121 – U2 ... 00701508 / $17.99
VOL. 122 – CROSBY, STILLS & NASH ... 00701610 / $16.99
VOL. 123 – LENNON & McCARTNEY ACOUSTIC ... 00701614 / $16.99
VOL. 124 – SMOOTH JAZZ ... 00200664 / $17.99
VOL. 125 – JEFF BECK ... 00701687 / $19.99
VOL. 126 – BOB MARLEY ... 00701701 / $17.99
VOL. 127 – 1970s ROCK ... 00701739 / $17.99
VOL. 129 – MEGADETH ... 00701741 / $17.99
VOL. 130 – IRON MAIDEN ... 00701742 / $17.99
VOL. 131 – 1990s ROCK ... 00701743 / $14.99
VOL. 132 – COUNTRY ROCK ... 00701757 / $15.99
VOL. 133 – TAYLOR SWIFT ... 00701894 / $16.99
VOL. 135 – MINOR BLUES ... 00151350 / $17.99
VOL. 136 – GUITAR THEMES ... 00701922 / $14.99
VOL. 137 – IRISH TUNES ... 00701966 / $17.99
VOL. 138 – BLUEGRASS CLASSICS ... 00701967 / $17.99
VOL. 139 – GARY MOORE ... 00702370 / $1
VOL. 140 – MORE STEVIE RAY VAUGHAN ... 00702396 / $2
VOL. 141 – ACOUSTIC HITS ... 00702401 / $1
VOL. 142 – GEORGE HARRISON ... 00237697 / $1
VOL. 143 – SLASH ... 00702425 / $1
VOL. 144 – DJANGO REINHARDT ... 00702531 / $1
VOL. 145 – DEF LEPPARD ... 00702532 / $1
VOL. 146 – ROBERT JOHNSON ... 00702533 / $1
VOL. 147 – SIMON & GARFUNKEL ... 14041591 / $1
VOL. 148 – BOB DYLAN ... 14041592 / $1
VOL. 149 – AC/DC HITS ... 14041593 / $1
VOL. 150 – ZAKK WYLDE ... 02501717 / $1
VOL. 151 – J.S. BACH ... 02501730 / $1
VOL. 152 – JOE BONAMASSA ... 02501751 / $2
VOL. 153 – RED HOT CHILI PEPPERS ... 00702990 / $2
VOL. 155 – ERIC CLAPTON UNPLUGGED ... 00703085 / $1
VOL. 156 – SLAYER ... 00703770 / $1
VOL. 157 – FLEETWOOD MAC ... 00101382 / $1
VOL. 159 – WES MONTGOMERY ... 00102593 / $2
VOL. 160 – T-BONE WALKER ... 00102641/ $1
VOL. 161 – THE EAGLES ACOUSTIC ... 00102659 / $1
VOL. 162 – THE EAGLES HITS ... 00102667 / $1
VOL. 163 – PANTERA ... 00103036 / $1
VOL. 164 – VAN HALEN: 1986-1995 ... 00110270 / $1
VOL. 165 – GREEN DAY ... 00210343 / $1
VOL. 166 – MODERN BLUES ... 00700764 / $1
VOL. 167 – DREAM THEATER ... 00111938 / $2
VOL. 168 – KISS ... 00113421 / $1
VOL. 169 – TAYLOR SWIFT ... 00115982 / $1
VOL. 170 – THREE DAYS GRACE ... 00117337 / $1
VOL. 171 – JAMES BROWN ... 00117420 / $1
VOL. 172 – THE DOOBIE BROTHERS ... 00119670 / $1
VOL. 173 – TRANS-SIBERIAN ORCHESTRA ... 00119907 / $1
VOL. 174 – SCORPIONS ... 00122119 / $1
VOL. 175 – MICHAEL SCHENKER ... 00122127 / $1
VOL. 176 – BLUES BREAKERS WITH JOHN MAYALL & ERIC CLAPTON ... 00122132 / $1
VOL. 177 – ALBERT KING ... 00123271 / $1
VOL. 178 – JASON MRAZ ... 00124165 / $1
VOL. 179 – RAMONES ... 00127073 / $1
VOL. 180 – BRUNO MARS ... 00129706 / $1
VOL. 181 – JACK JOHNSON ... 00129854 / $1
VOL. 182 – SOUNDGARDEN ... 00138161 / $1
VOL. 183 – BUDDY GUY ... 00138240 / $1
VOL. 184 – KENNY WAYNE SHEPHERD ... 00138258 / $1
VOL. 185 – JOE SATRIANI ... 00139457 / $1
VOL. 186 – GRATEFUL DEAD ... 00139459 / $1
VOL. 187 – JOHN DENVER ... 00140839 / $1
VOL. 188 – MÖTLEY CRÜE ... 00141145 / $1
VOL. 189 – JOHN MAYER ... 00144350 / $1
VOL. 190 – DEEP PURPLE ... 00146152 / $1
VOL. 191 – PINK FLOYD CLASSICS ... 00146164 / $1
VOL. 192 – JUDAS PRIEST ... 00151352 / $1
VOL. 193 – STEVE VAI ... 00156028 / $1
VOL. 194 – PEARL JAM ... 00157925 / $1
VOL. 195 – METALLICA: 1983-1988 ... 00234291 / $2
VOL. 196 – METALLICA: 1991-2016 ... 00234292 / $1

Prices, contents, and availability subject to change without notic

www.halleonard.com